I0049337

"Michael McCathren's book, The 6Ps of innovation provides managers and leaders with a deep, practical resource. Each of these six essential elements is illustrated by clear examples and fleshed out with ready-to-use tools and practices. Michael's book is designed for the hands-on Innovation practitioner who needs answers to the following questions: 'Where am I at? Where do I want to go? What should I do next? What should I avoid?'

— MICHAEL BARRY,
Adjunct Professor in the Mechanical Engineering Department at Stanford University (d.School), Founder of Quotient Design Research

"The applied nature of the book, including proven techniques and tools, will make it essential for all leaders who not only want to think about innovation but want to put innovation into action!"

— DAVID SUTHERLAND, PHD,
Senior Lecturer, The University of Georgia

"This highly practical book will be of immediate use to anyone lucky enough to take on a corporate innovation mandate. McCathren's book is brimming with easy-to-implement tools and techniques to apply that will bring clarity and focus to innovation efforts. This book will be helpful inspiration for anyone in a corporate innovation role or who has wondered how well their company rates on the questions: 'Are we doing the right things?' and 'Are we doing things right?'"

— BRIAN HINDO,
Partner, Innosight

"The 6Ps of Innovation is a comprehensive model for current and future business leaders who want to break away from traditional thinking to create an innovation organization. Both the "how" and the "why" are described with actionable detail making it easy for any reader to adopt the ideas presented. After practicing innovation for the majority of my career, I can highly recommend following the advice McCathren provides.

— AMIE GRAY,
CEO, NE Innovation

"Michael offers practical, experience-based principles for building a well-organized innovation culture that involves the right people in the appropriate roles and ultimately results in a more resilient organization."

— ALEX GONZALEZ,
Chief Innovation Officer of the Metro Atlanta Chamber and Author of Disruptor: How to Challenge the Status Quo and Unlock Innovation

"Having read numerous of innovation theory books, studied innovation at numerous junctures, and developed innovation systems for many organizations, I can clearly state that this work is simply the best I have seen. Michael has a comprehensive lens here and covers almost every single facet of what any innovation leader needs to both consider and master."

— DON ABRAHAM,
Senior Partner, Kantar

6P$_S$

OF

ESSENTIAL
INNOVATION

CREATE THE CULTURE AND CAPABILITIES OF A
RESILIENT INNOVATION ORGANIZATION

MICHAEL MCCATHREN

Copyright © 2022 by Ripples Media

All rights reserved. No part of this book may be reproduced or used in any manner without written permission of the copyright owner except for the use of quotations in a book review. For more information: contact@ripples.media

First printing 2022

Book design by Najdan Mancic

ISBN 979-8-9853234-1-2 Paperback
ISBN 979-8-9853234-0-5 Ebook

Published by Ripples Media
www.ripples.media

This book is the convergence of three love stories. The first is my love for creating and innovating. There is always a better way to think, do, and be. The second is the love story my wife Dena and I have been living since we met when we were three years old. She has been relentlessly loving me even when I should have been thinking, doing, and being better for her, for our kids, and our family. The third is the love story my Creator has been telling since the beginning of time. He is The Way to think, do, and be. He longs for me to spend eternity with Him and has provided a way through Christ, who makes it possible. "See what great love the Father has lavished on us, that we should be called children of God!" (1 John 3:1[NIV])

Sometimes we come across something so profoundly meaningful that it changes our course. Scott D. Anthony's *Little Black Book of Innovation: How It Works, How to Do It* marked a point in my life where my professional trajectory was altered forever and ignited in me an insatiable passion for innovation. If my words might impact someone, just one person, as deeply as Anthony's work has impacted me, I surely will have achieved my purpose as a professional and a teacher.

This book would not have happened if it were not for the inspiration and encouragement of Woody F. Faulk. Experiencing his leadership at Chick-fil-A has positively influenced my life far beyond my role in Innovation & New Ventures, and for that, I am deeply grateful.

CONTENTS

INTRODUCTION

There is no more "future-proofing." The future is happening too fast. There is only preparedness.

We do not know what tomorrow has in store for our businesses and our organizations. We formulate plans for possible scenarios that might guide our decisions should this or that scenario come to fruition. We cannot, however, plan for every scenario. I argue that we cannot plan for any scenario because we simply do not know what will happen tomorrow, next year, or in five years. Having a collection of scenario plans is not enough. The key to organizational resilience is to be adaptable and flexible with any disruption that may come our way.

In 2021, Deloitte published its *2021 Global Resilience Report*, which surveyed 2,260 CXOs in twenty-one countries. Deloitte found that companies with a few core attributes are better positioned to overcome disruptions and help usher in a "better normal."

Prepared was the attribute that topped the list.

➤ **Prepared**. "Successful CXOs plan for all outcomes, both short—and long-term. More than 85 percent of CXOs whose organizations successfully balanced addressing short—and long-term priorities felt they had pivoted very effectively to adapt to the events of 2020; fewer than half of organizations without that balance felt the same."

Next on the list were Adaptable, Collaborative, and Trustworthy.

➤ **Adaptable**. "Leaders recognize the importance of having versatile employees, especially after a year like 2020. To that end, flexibility/adaptability was, by far, the workforce trait CXOs said was most critical to their organizations' futures."

➤ **Collaborative**. "CXOs indicated the importance of collaboration within their organizations, noting that it sped decision-making, mitigated risk, and led to more innovation. Two-thirds of respondents who said their companies removed silos in their organizations before the pandemic reported managing the events of 2020 better than their peers."

➤ **Trustworthy**. "CXOs understand the challenge of building trust with key stakeholders, yet many did not feel they had lived up to the task. More than a third of respondents were not confident their organizations had maintained trust between leaders and employees."[1]

I noticed that "prepared" however, was not clearly defined in terms of actionable steps leaders could take to make their organizations more resilient. It made sense in my mind that these attributes represent variables in an equation the sum of which is **Preparedness**. Prepared, therefore is defined in terms of the presence and strength of adaptability, collaboration, and trustworthiness within an organization.

Prepared = Adaptable + Collaborative + Trustworthy

The secret to becoming a prepared organization is to be an innovation organization. Becoming an innovation organization will help ensure its resilience. This concept is the primary focus of this book presented as a journey through the *6 Ps of Essential Innovation.*

CONTEXT

The setting for this book lies in the reciprocal relationship between change and disruption. We are in a constant cycle of change and disruption because change creates disruption, and disruption creates change.

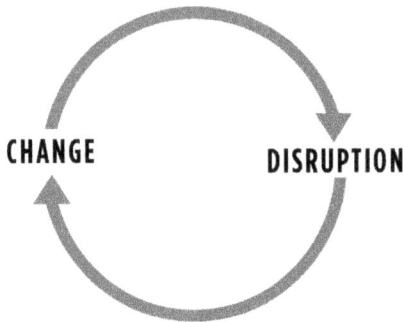

CHANGE   DISRUPTION

To varying degrees, change or disruption is happening right now in your organization. How well is your company currently dealing with the change that disruption is causing or the disruption that change is causing? Will your organization be prepared for what is coming next given that the nature, size, and scope of what is around the corner is unknown? Time will tell. But one thing is for certain, preparedness is the key.

Be the change, or be changed.

This book is both a blueprint and a field guide. Each of the six Ps of essential innovation acts as a building block constructed together in the order presented in the text. Depending on how developed the innovation culture and capabilities are within your organization, this construction effort can take up to three years.

6 Ps of Essential Innovation is not only an instruction manual for activating innovation capabilities, it is also a journey map intended to enhance and, in some cases, reshape an organization's culture. Any time culture shifts are involved, the work takes time and a long-term commitment of leadership. Approaching a book like *6 Ps of Essential Innovation* with the expectation that the seeds sown from its pages will bear fruit in only a few months is unrealistic. Although there will be many positive outcomes in the near term, a three-year prospective is recommended to make the internal strides necessary for transformation of this nature to take root and thrive on its own into the future.

HOW TO USE THIS BOOK

This book presents the six Ps of essential innovation in a specific order. The first three Ps relate to **culture**. Ps four through six relate to **capabilities**. There is no need to pursue embedding innovation capabilities into your organization if the culture is not ready to receive them. Thus, it is critical that the culture Ps be addressed first.

Essential Innovation is not a collection of theories that leave the application up to the reader to figure out. Each chapter presents specific concepts and provides suggestions on how to apply them right where you are. Each chapter discusses a specific "P" and concludes with a summary and a "Your Move" section.

"Your Move" questions give you the opportunity to reflect and react to the chapter learnings and then make actionable plans that are practical next steps. This book can be used for individual consumption or as a tool for teams to explore together, making the concepts applicable at scale.

WHY THIS BOOK?

I believe the most important questions are:

Are we doing the right things?
Are we doing things right?

These are deceptively simple questions, and the most difficult to answer for many organizations at any level. The answers to these questions represent the difference between organizations that flourish and those that flounder. The best right answers to these questions have eluded the most capable leaders, evaded the most progressive organizations, and frustrated the plans of the best high-performing teams. How confident are you that you already have the best right answers to these questions? How sure are you that your leaders know how to answer them well?

6 Ps of Essential Innovation provides pathways, strategies, and tools that lead to well-formulated answers to these questions, not just once, but from now on, and can help you transform your organization into a healthy and resilient innovation organization.

6 Ps OF ESSENTIAL INNOVATION

1

PERCEPTION

"Culture guides discretionary behavior, and it picks up where the employee handbook leaves off. Culture tells us how to respond to an unprecedented service request. It tells us whether to risk telling our bosses about our new ideas, and whether to surface or hide problems. Employees make hundreds of decisions on their own every day, and culture is our guide. Culture tells us what to do when the CEO isn't in the room, which is of course most of the time."

—FRANCES X. FREI AND ANNE MORRISS

Stephen R. Covey, author of *The 7 Habits of Highly Effective People*, wrote, "to change ourselves effectively, we first had to change our perceptions." As individuals, we have to be able to step outside of our contexts from which we operate routinely and acquire a less-biased vantage point on who we are and why we do what we do. The same is true for organizations, but in a more dramatic way. The collective perception of the members of an organization fuels its common beliefs, which drive individual behaviors, which ultimately defines the culture of the organization itself.

Is your organization innovative?
Does your organization have a culture of innovation?

Creating a culture that is effectively and sustainably innovative begins with changing how individuals throughout all levels of the organization *perceive* innovation—how it is defined, how it works, and what it does. That is why gaining an understanding of how you, your leadership, and staff perceive innovation at your organization is so critical. A baseline definition of what innovation currently means at your organization must be established before you can begin the journey of building a culture of innovation beyond it.

This chapter provides tools that will help you create a blueprint for creating a culture of innovation. Creating a culture of innovation is a long, multi-year journey and this material will only be as useful as the trust you place in the process. The tendency to rush through this discovery phase and to assign your own biases and assumptions must be avoided at all costs. A *culture* of innovation must be formed before the *capability* of innovation can be introduced.

Mark Fields, former CEO of Ford Motor Company said, "You can have the best plan in the world, and if the culture isn't going to allow it to happen, it's going to die on the vine."

INNOVATION PERCEPTION ASSESSMENT

In 2020, Innovation Leader (now InnoLead) surveyed 270 corporate leaders and posed the question: What tactics do corporate innovators feel create and support a culture of innovation?

Here is what they found:

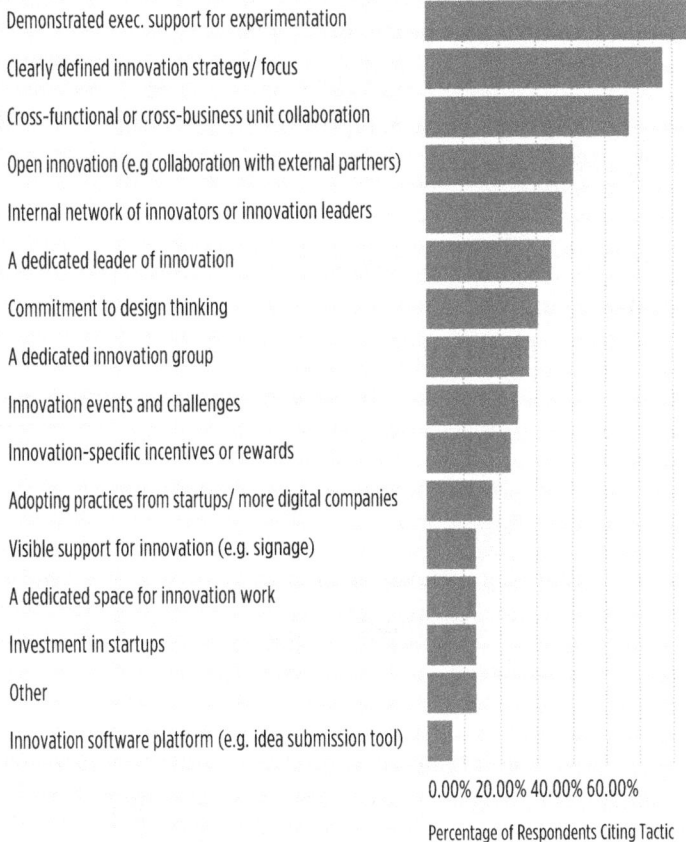

INNOVATION TACTICS BY INDUSTRY

Which of these things are most important to creating an innovative culture?

Tactic

- Demonstrated exec. support for experimentation
- Clearly defined innovation strategy/ focus
- Cross-functional or cross-business unit collaboration
- Open innovation (e.g collaboration with external partners)
- Internal network of innovators or innovation leaders
- A dedicated leader of innovation
- Commitment to design thinking
- A dedicated innovation group
- Innovation events and challenges
- Innovation-specific incentives or rewards
- Adopting practices from startups/ more digital companies
- Visible support for innovation (e.g. signage)
- A dedicated space for innovation work
- Investment in startups
- Other
- Innovation software platform (e.g. idea submission tool)

0.00% 20.00% 40.00% 60.00%

Percentage of Respondents Citing Tactic

Wouldn't it be interesting to see how your organization performs across all these dimensions? Understanding to what degree your staff perceives their organization is accomplishing each of these tactics is the essential first step in your journey to becoming an innovation organization.

To help acquire this understanding, start with the free Innovation Perception Assessment available at www.essential-innovation.com. You may send the link to as many people as you wish. It is critical that a representative sample be taken across all levels of your organization from the most senior to the most junior. If your organization employs more than 100 people, a good rule of thumb is to collect a total of 30 assessments spread across all levels. If there are more than 100 people within departments, collect 30 assessments from each department. A basic report is generated that will provide a good idea of your staff's perception of innovation.

> **Before you begin:** Take a moment and assume the mind of an unknowing beginner, a naïve investigator. Kill your inner expert. This is a theme that will be repeated throughout the book. When we think we know everything, we have stopped learning. You are about to have the enviable opportunity of learning how your staff perceives innovation. Do not assign meaning to the data. Let it speak for itself. To achieve this level of openness, forget everything you know about everything you know, and you will discover the truth faster.

The point of this assessment is to establish a baseline for where your organization is today in terms of being innovative, as perceived by your staff. The scoring is compiled across four pillars:

1. **Senior Leadership Pillar:** Examines how staff view the innovation behaviors of departmental and senior leaders. Title will be important so you can slice the data into senior leaders versus the rest of the staff. This will also help you understand how leaders view each other.

2. **Staff Pillar:** Provides staff with the opportunity to evaluate the degree to which they believe they are empowered and equipped to innovate.

3. **Culture Pillar:** Evaluates the extent to which beliefs and behaviors of a healthy innovation culture are present in the organization.

4. **Sustainability Pillar:** Examines the role that innovation plays in exploring and planning future growth opportunities.

Each pillar represents areas of your organization that are critical to creating and sustaining an innovation organization. The questions under each pillar are designed to surface insights that reveal what is currently driving or inhibiting your organization's progress on its innovation development journey. Analysis consists of a comprehensive score that describes your organization as Ailing, Moderate, or Fit in its innovation culture and capabilities across departments and titles. The report helps identify gaps such as people leaders' inability to lead with an innovation mindset, lack of tools that equip staff to apply innovation effectively, foresight versus myopia, the appetite for learning through experimentation, and much more.

THE SCORING RUBRIC

Weak

Innovation capabilities are underdeveloped across one or more pillars preventing an innovation practice from fully developing. The opportunity is to develop a strategic plan that establishes basic principles and practices from innovation across pillars.

Moderate

Medium-to-low scores are present within at least one pillar indicating gaps exist in these areas. While there are medium to high scores in some areas, these lower scores place organizational drag on the progress towards becoming a fully developed innovation organization. The opportunity is to define the gaps and develop a strategic plan to close them while maintaining current momentum in the key drivers of the higher scores.

Strong

No low scores exist within any pillar. The opportunity is to optimize engagement and to continually improve the organization's ability to lead with an innovation mindset and to apply innovation principles in its everyday operations.

To illustrate how straightforward the Innovation Perception Assessment much more can be, an assessment conducted with a large manufacturing company, which we'll call Lahebner, yielded the following findings.

STAFF PILLAR

We specifically recruit innovation-minded thinkers to join our organization

3

0 — 5

I feel equipped with the tools and resources I need to effectively apply the innovation process to my work

3.02

0 — 5

I have many opportunities to collaborate with anyone across the orgranization

3.9

0 — 5

How well I apply the innovation process is part of my performance assessment

2.4

0 — 5

I have been trained on how to apply the innovation process

1.95

0 — 5

I know what my thinking style is

3.7

0 — 5

I receive ongoing development that increases my innovation acumen

2.33

0 — 5

My leader allows me to explore ideas that are not part of my everyday role

3.85

0 — 5

I am given enough time to fully complete each stage of the innovation process

2.05

0 — 5

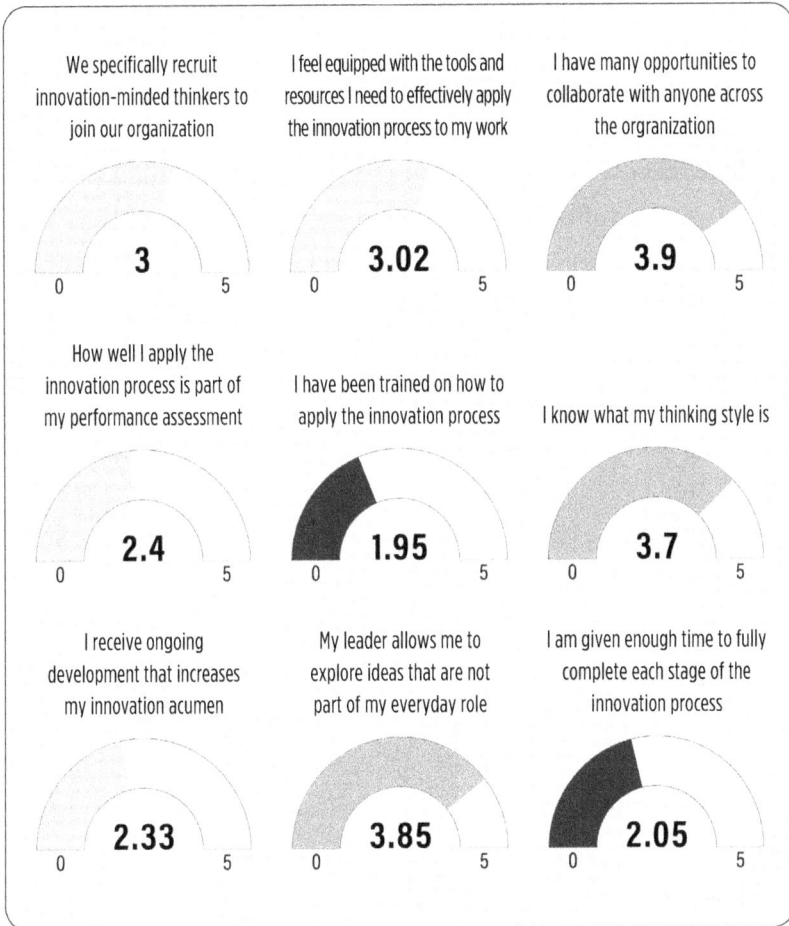

Regarding the Staff Pillar, you will notice gray and black scores. These represent gaps or areas for improvement. Executives discovered there were two deficiencies at Lahebner:

➤ Knowledge of the innovation process
➤ Understanding of how to apply it to everyday work

We will address the latter first. Although collaboration, exploration, and thinking styles scored well, staff believed they had not been trained on how to apply the innovation process. They also believed they did not have enough time to complete each stage of the innovation process.

The scores suggest that leaders at Lahebner should focus on these two areas of deficiency if they hope to become a resilient innovation organization. It is not enough that staff are merely aware of the innovation process. Without knowing how to apply the innovation process and allowing enough time to apply it well, innovation will not become a capability at Lahebner. There is a significant difference between education (knowing the innovation process) and application (turning ideas into value).

In this case, Lahebner implemented an innovation coaches program. Volunteers from several departments agreed to be trained on how to coach others so they too will be equipped with how to apply the innovation process. What they discovered was that as more staff became skilled in applying the innovation process, it became more apparent that to do it well requires time. Once leaders became aware of this investment need, they allowed more time in project plans to conduct each step of their innovation process more thoroughly. This time need was especially true for the iterative process of prototyping (more on that in the "Process" chapter). It may seem counterintuitive, but taking the necessary time in the first part of the innovation process allows the project to move faster in the back half.

The outcome for Lahebner was that more project teams were able to develop better solutions faster and launch them with fewer problems.

CULTURE PILLAR

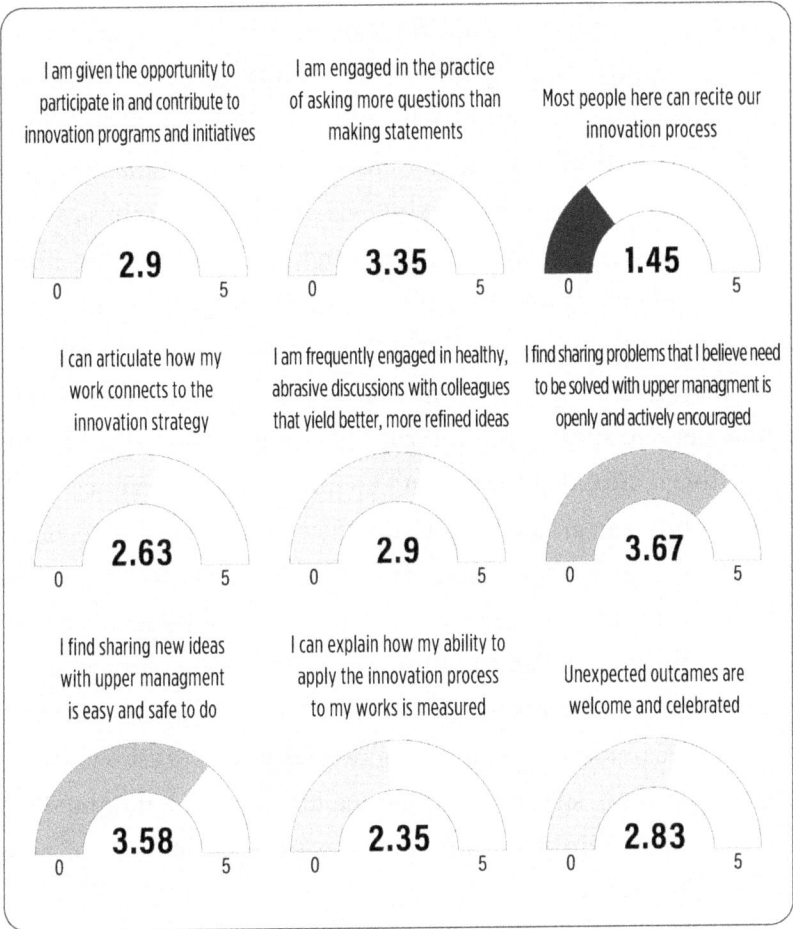

I am given the opportunity to participate in and contribute to innovation programs and initiatives

2.9
0 — 5

I am engaged in the practice of asking more questions than making statements

3.35
0 — 5

Most people here can recite our innovation process

1.45
0 — 5

I can articulate how my work connects to the innovation strategy

2.63
0 — 5

I am frequently engaged in healthy, abrasive discussions with colleagues that yield better, more refined ideas

2.9
0 — 5

I find sharing problems that I believe need to be solved with upper managment is openly and actively encouraged

3.67
0 — 5

I find sharing new ideas with upper managment is easy and safe to do

3.58
0 — 5

I can explain how my ability to apply the innovation process to my works is measured

2.35
0 — 5

Unexpected outcames are welcome and celebrated

2.83
0 — 5

As stated earlier, the survey revealed that the other deficiency at Lahebner was that staff were unable to recite the organization's innovation process, as you see in the meter in black below. The score suggests that innovation is not a topic that staff hear leaders talk about often. Innovation's importance in everyday work is likely not modeled by senior leaders, so staff are not held accountable to make thinking innovatively part of their routine.

Change and disruption can hit cultures like this particularly hard. When unforeseen forces require the organization to think in new ways, it catches leaders and staff off balance; unprepared to optimize the opportunity. They must then abruptly learn innovation in a reactionary setting which usually does not create meaningful results. If instead, staff were already trained and routinely approached their work with an innovative mindset within a culture that encourages innovation, change and disruption are less likely to have a shocking effect. Staff in an innovation organization can more effectively pivot to exploring new, high-quality ideas quickly.

Also notice the significant presence of gray scores. Overall, Lahebner had specific cultural gaps that must be addressed before any effort is allocated to standing up innovation capabilities.

The first step in rectifying the deficiencies is to understand all the possible causes for these results. For example, why haven't staff been trained on the innovation process? Why are they not able to recite it?

The Innovation Perception Assessment points to strengths and weaknesses but understanding the root cause of them is the real value of this endeavor. By isolating two key results (as shown in the diagram below), specific plans can be developed to address these gaps and can help point attention toward specific areas of root cause investigation.

I have been trained on how to
apply the innovation process

1.95

0   5

STAFF PILLAR

Most people here can recite our
innovation process

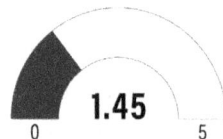

1.45

0   5

CULTURE PILLAR

In this case, further investigation found there was not a formal innovation process at all at Lahebner. Different departments pieced together versions of a process, but there was no common process or language across the company. This is the type of insight that can help organizations map their journey toward becoming an innovation organization in the most efficient and effective way possible. If you are starting from a place of "Weak," or having no formalized innovation capabilities at all, these gaps will be important points to which a disproportionate amount of attention should be given before launching innovation at your organization.

In some cases, assessment results may push leaders to consider the core assumptions under which their organization has operated for years. This proposition can be challenging for organizations for three reasons. First, with age comes rigidity. The older an organization, the less likely it is to embrace the idea of evolving its culture. This reticence can be due to deeply rooted hierarchies and complex relationship systems. Second, success can breed complacency. When times are good, organizations are reluctant to introduce self-inflicted change. On the other hand, when times are challenging, the tendency is to eliminate any initiatives that are not essential to sustaining the current business model, even when a new business model may very well lead the company out of the valley of hardship and into prosperity. Third, legacy mindsets are difficult to change.

When leaders have been in position for a long time, they naturally default to the leadership and decision-making system on which they have always depended. An assessment that suggests a shift in culture is necessary to become an innovation organization challenges existing decision-making systems. This usually introduces the idea that cultural shifts are necessary which can threaten legacy leaders' long-held positions.

REALITY CHECK

Because actively learning and understanding new things are the basic building blocks of any innovation organization, every leader must be open to the feedback from this survey. The Innovation Health Assessment reflects how well your staff believes you are doing when it comes to innovation, and the scores may sting a bit. If you are not willing and able to accept criticism with a welcoming spirit of continuous improvement, then chances are you have a culture that is also unwilling and unable to accept the adaptability, collaboration, and trustworthiness that comes with being an innovation organization. Said differently, if the culture is not ready to accept innovation, it could be because the members of its culture do not believe the leaders are truly ready to accept innovation.

Followers take behavioral cues from their leaders, particularly when it comes to innovation. If you want your organization to be innovative, it is up to you to model innovation behaviors such as curiosity, counter-intuitive thinking, mining for unusual ideas, and inviting suggestions for new directions (just to name a few), even if it means your own potential blind spots and shortcomings will be laid bare.

You must also be willing to protect the constructs of innovation itself and defend it against competing priorities of core business initiatives. In the words of Vijay Govindarajan and Chris Trimble, authors of *The Other Side of Innovation* [2], "Organizations are not designed for innovation. Quite the contrary, they are designed for ongoing operations."

Designing your organization for innovation could require that part of your role becomes ensuring a balance between managing the present work of the core organization with forging a future through innovation.

The world around us is changing so rapidly, standing still is moving backward.

Unpredictable circumstances deal many organizations crushing blows by imposing sudden change. When it comes to change, there are two types of organizations. On the one hand, non-innovative organizations are only able to formulate some sort of reaction to changes and hope that the rate of external change does not outpace their ability to eventually change internally. Change in these types of organizations, even on a small scale, becomes a disruption, which becomes a distraction for leadership. What follows are inefficiencies in leading people that then create a poor employee experience, which leads to inefficient execution, which leads to poor customer experience, all causing the organization to painfully, reactively retool and rebuild or wither and die altogether.

On the other hand, there are organizations that have a healthy innovation culture and welcome change, can thrive through disruption with agility and flexibility, and seek opportunities to push positive forces of change into the world in surprising ways. The Innovation Health Assessment helps leaders realize which type of organization they are leading.

WHEN IS THE RIGHT TIME TO START?

Although the results of the Innovation Health Assessment may convince you that your organization should become a developing innovation organization, the question is: Are you ready? At some point, the growth of your organization will reach an inflection point where the rate of growth will begin to decrease at an increasing rate. Over time, if unattended, growth will eventually flatten, then decline. Your aim as a leader should be to push the inflection point as far out into the future as possible. The way to shift the inflection point is through constantly innovating. This could sound like an ominous task unless yours is an innovation organization. If that is true, then constantly innovating is not only an everyday mode of working, it is who you are as an organization.

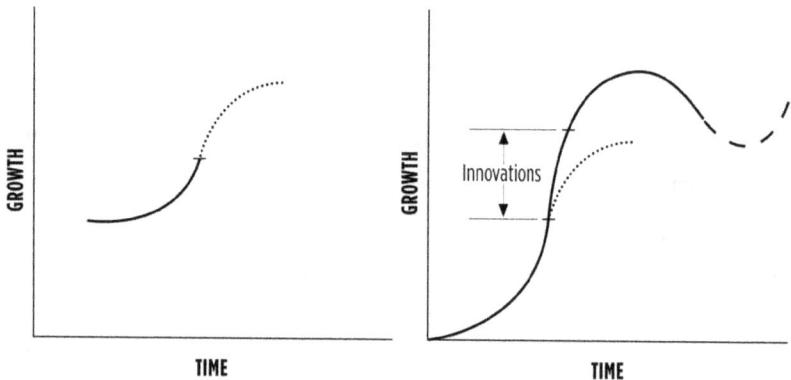

Many organizations find themselves in the first section of the curve, before the inflection point. In this section of the curve, most resources can be consumed by supporting the current demands of the company and the challenges that come with managing day-to-day activities. If this is you, it may not be the right time to dive into the deep end of the organizational transformation pool. Transformation of this nature requires broad support from the organization's highest leaders. If there is no room on upper management's agenda for becoming an innovation organization, then you may be more effective planting the seeds of essential innovation by conducting ongoing, intentional conversations with key stakeholders until your organization reaches a point where it can give some of its attention to your transformational initiatives.

Shifts of this nature will take time and there is no time like the present. It will also need a champion for the cause. Perhaps there is no one better suited to create innovation momentum where you are than you!

➤ There is no such thing as an innovative company. How healthy the culture of innovation is within each sub-department collectively determines how innovative a company is. Getting this right at the sub-department level is key.

➤ Change is permanent. Its velocity is increasing, and the stakes are higher than ever. Do you confidently and methodically lead through disruptions or suffer through them? Do your behaviors and language consistently demonstrate your commitment to embrace change and see it as a source of fuel rather than a source of fear?

➤ When it comes to innovation, is your organization Weak, Moderate, or Strong? Becoming an innovation organization requires an honest analysis of how innovative your staff perceives your organization to be. If your staff were asked today, would they define innovation in a consistent way, and agree unanimously that your organization is an innovative organization?

➤ Evolving into something new means evolving away from something old. Are there specific assumptions about how your organization currently operates that should be left behind to open new opportunities for growth?

YOUR MOVE

🧠 REFLECTION:

How have you contributed to creating an innovation organization? What do you believe is the best opportunity for you to serve your organization that would improve its scores?

💬 REACTION:

What did you find surprising (positively and negatively) about the scores? What are the root causes behind the lowest scores?

🎯 ACTION:

What conversations about these results will you have and with whom? What short-term and long-term outcomes do you hope these conversations will accomplish? Who will help you achieve these outcomes?

2

PEOPLE

"65 percent of failures are due to people problems."

—NOAM WASSERMAN,

The Founder's Dilemma

Innovation is often viewed by leaders as someone else's job. It's everyone's job!

For years, there has been debate whether sustainable value-add innovation is the result of a faultless innovation process or talented, highly creative **people**. The most common conclusion is that it takes both, to varying degrees, depending on the business or operating model. Take Intel for example. The company tends to be more process-heavy because of the precise technical nature of its business. On the other hand, Pixar places slightly more importance on highly creative thinkers. What about your organization? Should the scale tip more toward process or people?

Let's consider a typical organizational operating model. An organization commonly has vision, mission, and value statements penned by a few senior leaders who are accountable to a board or committee. The typical company is organized into departments, each headed by a people leader. Each leader creates a vision statement for their department that hopefully ladders up to the company's strategic goals within its business framework. The vision of each leader is translated into initiatives that are managed and executed by their staff. Stringing all these factors together forms the operating model of the departments and ultimately the entire company. Does that sound like it slants toward process or people? Except for creating and casting the vision, everything else basically becomes process management. In many departments, there is one person with the vision, and everyone executes it.

In marketplace circles, this management model would be called "command and control" and in some cases, marketplace results of these organizations trail those that are innovation organizations. At the highest level, evolving into an innovation organization involves flipping the traditional management model on its head and creating a culture that unleashes the power of its people to creatively solve problems more autonomously.

This flip begins with you and other leaders. Hopefully, you have found this book to be inspiring so far, but this is the point of our journey when some leaders decide they would rather not enter a space of frank self-evaluation and raw reflection. This chapter requires honest introspection and deals with the realities of leading with the innovation mindset and creating an innovation organization.

I recall one leader, whom we will call "Jordan". She was hired by a large organization to lead its public relations department. She was brilliant and had an impressive track record. She was at the top of her game when she joined the company. After only a few months on the job, I could tell she was struggling. Her boss was trying to manage a fast and furious workload himself and did not provide much guidance. His only direction was—"Be innovative!!" She immersed herself in formulating strategy and calling shots. Her team was frustrated by her absence and lack of accessibility. Let us look at how Jordan's leadership style stifled her team's innovation and placed a lid on the impact she and her team had on the business.

The authors of *The Innovator's DNA*[3] state that "roughly two-thirds of our innovation skills still come through learning—from first understanding the skill, then practicing it, and ultimately gaining confidence in our capacity to create." The skills they describe as building blocks for innovative thinking are not the skills most education institutions provide. Consider your own college experience. Was there a degree in creative problem solving or a college of innovation? Many institutions teach leadership from a process orientation. Yet, to be a resilient innovation organization, leaders must lead with an innovation mindset.

Leaders of the future will be required to lead with an innovation mindset, not a process mindset. This perspective requires a particular set of skills that anyone can acquire, but it requires intentionality, diligence, and practice.

In today's high-velocity culture, relying solely on decades-old leadership methods and practices is like walking backward into the future.

INNOVATION SKILLS

Questioning

From the time we took our first academic test, we began to learn that having the right answer earns the reward. We were groomed to look for the right answer and did not learn how to ask great questions. Over time, our curiosity died and questions evolved into what was perceived as evidence of our ignorance rather than our sincere desire to learn and understand more.

Let us look again at Jordan and focus specifically on her questioning skills. Jordan's track record was a series of solo accomplishments. She had managed several high-profile clients in the past and the photos on her office wall told the story of a driven, powerful woman. Jordan, like many leaders, believed she alone must be the idea generator. That notion is reinforced by most of today's company environments. The big-idea initiator gets promoted. Leaders have the ideas; employees do what they are told until it is their turn to have their own big ideas.

Jordan came into her role wanting to make a statement and to quickly establish her credibility as a capable leader. But she did not just make *a* statement, she made a great deal of them. In fact, when she spoke, she made nothing but statements. When Jordan met with her team, her peers, and her boss, she did a great deal of "telling." She stepped into the role as the expert and was incurious about existing team conditions, norms, accomplishments, plans, and capabilities. Jordan believed that if she asked a lot of questions, it might appear that she did not know what to do or how to do it. Yet questions are the means by which great things are accomplished. Asking great questions from a genuine spirit of curiosity is a fundamental innovation skill that Jordan lacked. There was no way she would be able to establish an innovation culture without asking many questions.

Future leaders will seek the right questions rather than the right answers.

Observing

We are trained to read directions carefully and follow the rules. Translation: observe what parents, teachers, coaches, instructors, and bosses tell us to do and treat these directed observations with great importance. When we are told to look at something a certain way, we tend to only look at it from that one perspective. We are trained to view the world around us from a single view. A brief look at the past reveals that those who changed history were people who viewed the world from many different perspectives. Leonardo da Vinci would reportedly sketch a subject from different angles before he attempted a final version so he could adequately capture the essence of the form from several different perspectives. His buddies laughed at him. When considering a subject, they all saw the same thing from the same perspective, but da Vinci saw something different. He became famous. How many of his buddies can you name?[4]

On one occasion, Jordan was part of a crisis management meeting with other marketing leaders. These meetings were frequent events where each leader would weigh in on the situation and recommend a course of action for his/her respective areas. They valued Jordan's perspective because of her vast experience in dealing with publicity crises. It didn't take long for them to notice that her approach was always the same. The lens through which she viewed each situation appeared to be the usual monocle she brought with her into this role. Jordan did not know how to gather all the inputs from a variety of perspectives, examine insights, determine all the various options, and enlist other viewpoints to help shape her ultimate recommendation. She was trapped in the singularity.

Observing, in this context, is the act of viewing a problem or opportunity from as many perspectives as possible, like da Vinci, to capture as much of the essence of a subject as possible so that it can be fully understood. Next, we will see how Jordan's independent approach and siloed decision-making make a culture of innovation almost impossible to create.

Multiplicity of perspectives will provide future leaders with deeper understanding, which leads to wisdom.

Networking

We naturally gravitate towards people with whom we share something in common. We have not been taught to break out of our homogeneous networks and to think differently about who could or should be a part of them. It may be discussed in institutes of higher learning, but *how* to do it is not clearly explained. Steve Jobs, Ed Catmull, and Alan Kay were innovators and inventors but were also all white guys who loved technology, production, and design. Hardly a network of diversity. Nonetheless, these are our examples. Entrepreneur and motivational speaker Jim Rohn penned, "You are the average of the five people we spend the most time with." We will discuss the importance of diverse perspectives later in this chapter.

In Jordan's situation, the lack of the most fundamental innovation skill–questioning–plus her unskilled observations were compounded by her personal network that was neither deep nor wide nor diverse. It is not uncommon for leaders to be so immersed in their work that they believe they cannot afford to carve out time to establish, build, and nurture relationship networks with people unlike themselves who will enhance and challenge their thinking.

If Jordan had such a network, she would likely understand the value of questions and might realize a single view is not an effective way to approach problems and ideas. Without it, she is left to her own devices and lone experiences to construct her own ideas. After a few months in her new role, Jordan shared with us that she felt like she was on a treadmill set at max speed at its top incline. By the time she celebrated her one-year anniversary, she was exhausted and had not moved anything forward. She had not done anything to create a culture of innovation. In fact, her behavior would suggest she did not understand the value that a culture of innovation could generate or how one was even established. Her team and her peers were beginning to wonder if Jordan was the wrong choice for this job.

Future leaders will possess the ability to activate higher-than-average innovation thinking through networks of people who represent multiple diverse perspectives, thus elevating the power of their innovation mindset.

Experimenting

In general, most leaders do very little experimenting. If you are like most leaders, you spend 90 percent of your time managing how not to fail, versus how to succeed. That focus is not an innovation mindset. Why don't more leaders do more experimenting? Because they have been taught that failure is bad. Failed experiments do not earn promotions or raises. You have achieved what you have in your career because you had the right answers and avoided failure. The right answers are sure. Experiments are risky. Thus, experimenting is too closely associated with failure and should be avoided if we want a bigger title. So traditional thinking goes.

Jordan was no different. Like most leaders in a fast-paced setting, she believed she did not have the luxury of experimenting with ideas and potential solutions. She certainly did not want anything her hands touched to be associated with failure. Jordan was trapped in "safe" mode. "Businesses do not move forward in "safe" mode. Organizations that make breakthrough advancements do so through breakthrough thinking. That type of thinking is borne of an innovation culture, where experimentation is encouraged and managing risk is an understood aspect of it.

In one situation, protestors had amassed around several of the company's distribution centers across the country. They were well-organized. There was a clear leader at each location with support teams that worked in shifts around the clock. They had garnered media coverage in almost every location. Jordan had seen this before. From her perspective and experience, the traditional approach was the best response, which was not directly engaging with the protestors. She crafted a statement for the media and did not address any communication directly to the protesting group. The problem was, Jordan's company had a long history of strong and healthy relationships with this protesting party and it did not feel very relational to other leaders to ignore them.

Future leaders will understand that experiments are not judged in terms of successes or failures, but on the merits of how well they searched for and eliminated "unexpected outcomes".

If Jordan possessed innovation skills, she would have immediately asked a great deal of questions from as many parties as possible, including the protestors. She would have observed that the company historically had a good relationship with this group. Perhaps her recommended course of action would have been different than what she had done in the past with other organizations. And if she had been a leader with an innovation mindset, she would have perhaps developed a more relational, conversational response and experimented with engaging with protestors at one location to see how they might respond.

Jordan would also learn from one engagement, refine her approach, and engage the next location with even better results. In the end, the outcome was a long and painfully public dispute. Jordan's predictable response was typical of tactics utilized by many other companies out there. There was nothing breakthrough about her approach and therefore the outcome was absent of any breakthroughs.

Unfortunately, this pattern continued until Human Resources intervened. Together, they developed a leadership development program designed to introduce Jordan to innovation skills as well as other leadership tools. In the meantime, her department experienced many team members who requested to move to other departments, while some left the company altogether. They were seeking an environment that was more inclusive and collaborative—the hallmarks of an innovation culture. Eventually, Jordan became a leader with an innovation mindset and began to create a culture of innovation within her department. The transformation was difficult. Shedding our mental models that have cured and hardened over many years takes time, but it can be done. Are you ready to begin your journey?

SHIFT THE FAILURE NARRATIVE

Building on the experimentation skill mentioned previously, it is necessary to address the fear of failing that is associated with experimentation. Fear of failure is present in all of us. It has been nurtured through each stage of our education and into our professional lives. No one gets promoted because of his or her failures. Failure is failure. Attempting to rewire our minds from "failure is bad" to "failure is good" is a waste of time and effort. Failure is bad. It always has been and it always will be. A culture of innovation will not take root in an environment where the fear of failure is stronger than the desire to adapt, collaborate, and trust one another.

The only way to overcome this counterproductive fear of failure is to shift the narrative away from failure to *unexpected outcomes*. Unlike failures, unexpected outcomes refine good ideas and transform them into great solutions. We should eagerly seek them out. They are the insights that point to specific areas that highlight how to make ideas better. On the other hand, focusing on failures highlights areas where the idea is lacking and not good enough. Many times, leaders internalize the failure of their idea and feel like they personally have failed. The result is that leaders avoid risk and experimentation, which are essential components of the innovation process. When leaders believe a failed idea is a reflection of their leadership abilities, a culture of innovation will not take root. Seeking unexpected outcomes, however, shifts the negative narrative of failure to a positive one based on the spirit of improvement rather than judgment.

The only "fail" in an innovator's vocabulary should be this:

F. A. I. L.

Forgetting
About the
Importance of
Learning

Another reason to shift the failure narrative has to do with the cost of the common catchphrase, "fail fast, fail often." This involves two parts. First, failing fast can often short circuit the benefits of iterative prototyping. Dan Pontefract wrote in a 2018 *Forbes* article titled "The Foolishness of Fail Fast, Fail Often," "When executives institute a 'fail fast, fail often' mantra, they must ensure it will not be at the expense of creative or critical thinking. Time is our most precious resource. When 'fail fast, fail often' is invoked, it cannot become a culture where speed trumps the time we need to spend on creativity. Furthermore, we must not become preoccupied to fail by preceding the requirement to make judicious, thoughtful decisions."

Second, there is a cumulative financial cost to failing. Over time, I believe investors become less interested in the company trying as many ideas as possible in hopes that a winning idea will surface as a financial success. This is what I call *idea-driven innovation*. Investors are, in a sense, paying for failures. It is more financially appealing to focus on the right audience to serve and choose the right problem to solve. I call this *audience-based innovation*. Investors are more interested in ensuring the company is allocating resources in pursuit of smarter, more strategic opportunities where they can win from a position of strength. Rather than pay for multiple failures, invest in exploring unexpected outcomes.[5]

WORKING WITH UNEXPECTED OUTCOMES

Unexpected outcomes come into play during prototyping. Once the solution is identified and is ready to move into prototyping, a list of expected outcomes should be compiled. During prototyping, a list should be compiled of the unexpected outcomes actually observed and compared to the expected outcomes list. For each unexpected outcome, its root cause should be fully understood so the correct refinements can be made with the next iteration. When there are no more unexpected outcomes, the idea is ready to move forward. This is discussed in detail in the Process chapter.

YOUR INNOVATION READINESS

Most leaders agree that an innovation capability can have a positive impact on their organizations. Many are inspired to be agents of positive change that might raise the level of performance and unleash the true potential that lies within their organizations. They are eager to share their good learnings from this book with receptive leaders in their company in hopes that they too might see the possibility and likewise be inspired to move forward toward becoming an innovation organization. All too often, however, their enthusiasm is met with lukewarm interest and insincere obligatory head nods from senior leaders. Why?

Why are so many senior leaders averse to learning how to create an innovation culture? Do they inherently have an aversion to innovation? They might believe they want their company to become an innovative organization. They might even agree that their company is not currently innovative but should be. And yet, they still do not make the building of innovation culture and capabilities a priority. Why? What is getting in the way?

They may have innovative thoughts but "being" innovative is like running on a treadmill—they spend a great deal of energy running but do not make any forward progress. You might not be able to sway others toward prioritizing innovation, but you can begin with what you have, right where you are. Your behavior can be contagious, and the results of your innovation practice will be undeniable. These might be the catalysts that spark a desire in other leaders to create an innovation culture right where they are too.

It is time to take a moment, look in the mirror, and do an honest evaluation of your willingness to create an innovation organization. If you honestly admit that your perspective on innovation should evolve and you feel compelled to become a leader who leads with an innovation mindset, then let us examine how that can be accomplished.

If you dove into this book as a leader who is hungry to build an innovation organization and who has already been swimming in innovation waters for some time, you are in the right place. If this is all new to you, then this is a great place to start. Regardless of how far along the journey you are to becoming a leader with an innovation mindset, and before you take the next step, let us evaluate your current organizational structure and the type of leadership mode you employ.

FORMS OF LEADING

What kind of leader are you? How have you designed the way your leadership is experienced by others? Typically, within many companies there are two forms of leading: autocracy and oligarchy. In the autocratic form, decisions are made by one person. Not routine everyday decisions, but higher-level issues such as strategic direction, branding, resources (human and dollars), how those resources are allocated, and the like. These are decisions that are left to the discretion of only one person. As the autocratic organization grows it creates "mini-autocracies" led by people who are the only ones who make decisions for their departments. While this is an efficient form of rule that significantly reduces time in meetings and the time it takes to make a decision, it is an entirely inefficient approach if the desire is breakthrough, transformational growth.

What is more undesirable is that the autocratic organization's ability to handle change and disruption is limited by the ability of only one person: its leader. Autocratic leaders likely do not possess the ability to innovate, to see blind spots, to take on alternative perspectives, and to listen to interestingly diverse people and understand their ideas. Adaptability, collaboration, and trustworthiness are essential attributes of a prepared organization; and they can be challenges within autocracies.

You may be a great visionary who has created and led a company into an expanding and thriving organization. And this is not a debate about your ability to lead. We simply need to point out that autocracies are most effective as long as the degree of external change is slight, and its pace is slow. The danger autocratic leaders face is that change is neither light nor slow in much of today's environments.

Furthermore, autocracies are like tribes. In tribes, there is one chief. When do chiefs know when it is time to step down because the needs of the tribe are greater than the original vision he once had for them? Answer: they don't! Chiefs are autocratic leaders with a limited sight distance and sometimes their thinking becomes obsolete. When it does, the tribe must deal with the reality that the chief must be removed. Removal of an unsuspecting autocratic figure can be a damaging season of change that stifles growth and sometimes destroys the organization altogether.

In an oligarchy, the rights to make decisions belong to only a few people at the top of the organization. The power resides within a tight group of people who likely look, talk, and think like each other and probably have similar life experiences and backgrounds. The leader who built this team must have a great deal of trust in its members, and therefore the team often becomes a homogenous group of "insiders."

Assembling an oligarchical team with the same values and worldviews may be helpful in some ways, but if those requisites, plus relevant work experience, are the only qualifications, then the oligarchic leadership team can unknowingly sow the seeds of decline because it will miss the valuable synergies of a diversified and inclusive management approach. Diversity is often seen as a challenge to the oligarch's power and a threat to its ability to ensure that the rank-and-file stay in line. If this describes your organization, you have unintentionally placed a lid on its potential to innovate, grow, and prosper long-term. You may want to explore the alternative.

I would like to encourage you to consider "flat-archy" as an alternative. Unlike traditional hierarchies, where ideas are typically expressed in one-way flows of communication and only those at the top have all the information and power, members of "flat-archies" find themselves looking left and right for collaboration, rather than up and down for instruction or command. As Jacob Morgan, a leading expert on the future of work, describes in his book, *The Future of Work: Attract New Talent, Build Better Leaders, and Create a Competitive Organization*, "A 'flatter' structure seeks to open up the lines of communication and collaboration while removing layers within the organization"—an essential element of an innovation organization.

How often do you work in teams in your job? According to a recent workplace survey conducted by Deloitte, only 38 percent of companies today are organized by functional role and that most companies are moving (or have already moved) to more decentralized, flexible team-based structures. This shift is particularly dramatic in the context of innovation. Teams of innovators need to represent a wide variety of skills and functional knowledge, but also need to be able to move quickly and to shift direction in response to new information.

—DR. BARBARA LARSON,
"The Human Side of Innovation" Northeastern University, 2021

According to Morgan, there are certain components necessary for a flatarchy to be effective.

➤ Employees need to be able to easily collaborate and access each other and information anywhere, anytime, from any device.

➤ Executives and managers need to understand that employees don't *need* to work at your company, they should *want* to work there and as a result, everything should be designed around that principle.

➤ Managers exist to support the employees, and not vice versa. This role also means that senior leaders focus on pushing the power of authority down to others instead of pushing down information and communication messages.

➤ The organization must accept that the way we work is changing and must therefore be comfortable with things like flexible work arrangements, getting rid of annual employee reviews, and challenging other outdated ways of working.

The point here is that there must be a culture established that is ready to accept innovation as a way of behaving. This is not about tearing the engine out of the plane mid-flight or changing the tires on a moving car. These are not wholesale changes that occur to the existing culture overnight. The emphasis here is the envisioning of a cultural transformation around how your organization thinks about what it does, relating more collaboratively with one another, acting more innovatively, and starting a proper innovation journey with a commitment to seeing it through.[6]

Gary P. Pisano of the Harvard Business School warns us to keep in mind that "Lack of hierarchy does not mean lack of leadership." He continues, "Paradoxically, flat organizations require stronger leadership than hierarchical ones. Flat organizations often devolve into chaos when leadership fails to set clear strategic priorities and directions." As organizations transform into flatarchies, it may require leaders to acquire a different skill set and a new set of tools. Instead of hammers and nails, leaders may need paint and drop cloths. When this change happens, they will only know how to use their new tools effectively when a clear connection is made between strategic priorities and the level of cross collaboration and inclusion that is required to bring the strategies to life.[7]

THE INCLUSIVE LEADER AND INNOVATION

"If you do not intentionally include, you unintentionally exclude."

—EKATERINA WALTER

Bernadette Dillon and Juliet Bourke, client director and partner, respectively, in Human Capital consulting at Deloitte, advise that diversity of thinking is a critical ingredient for effective collaboration. Far from being guided by hunches and feelings, or leaving success to chance, inclusive leaders adopt a disciplined approach to diversity of thinking, paying close attention to team composition and the decision-making processes employed. In this way, they understand the demographic factors that cause individuals and groups to think differently, both directly (educational background and mental frameworks) and indirectly (gender and race). They purposely align individuals to teams based on that knowledge. As mentioned previously, innovation is how we *think* about what we do, not merely *something* we do.

Bourke describes six traits of inclusive leadership: Commitment, Courage, Cognizance of bias, Curiosity, Cultural intelligence, and Collaboration. I want to focus on the sixth trait: **Collaboration**. Bourke identifies three key elements of collaboration and points out ways leaders think about collaboration, and then how they can bring collaboration to life through inclusive leadership actions.

SIGNATURE TRAIT: COLLABORATION		
Element	**What inclusive leaders think about**	**What inclusive leaders do**
Empowerment	• Ensuring that others feel able and comfortable to contribute independently	• Give team members the freedom to handle difficult situations • Empower team members to make decision about issues that impact their work • Hold team members accountable for performance they can control
Teaming	• Being disciplined about diversity of thinking in terms of team composition and processes	• Assemble teams that are diverse in thinking • Work hard to ensure that team members respect each other and that there are no out-groups within the team • Anticipate and take appropriate action to address team conflict when it occurs
Voice	• Adapting styles and processes to ensure that every team member has a voice	• Create a safe environment where people feel comfortable to speak up • Explicitly include all team members in discussions • Ask follow-up questions

https://www2.deloitte.com/us/en/insights/topics/talent/six-signature-traits-of-inclusive-leadership.html

I call your attention to two elements in particular: Empowerment and Voice. First, empowering your team to tackle problems on their own brings out their natural God-given ability to be creative problem solvers within a comfortable environment. In an innovation culture, each team member will naturally gather input from others as they go about solving their problem, thus fueling collaboration in ways that become routine behavior. "I'm invited by others to solve their challenges. Why wouldn't I do the same to solve mine?" That is how breakthrough solutions occur.

Second, an essential distinction needs to be made regarding Voice. Having a voice and being heard are two different concepts. Collaboration within a culture of innovation means that all voices carry equal weight. This balance is easier said than done.[8]

Jaime was leading a project developing a new product for commercial kitchens and was doing all the right things as a leader with an innovation mindset. Every week, the team met to discuss the project and each team member had ten minutes to provide an update and ask for input and ideas. As the team progressed through the innovation process, Jaime noticed most members would consistently take all ten minutes but one member, Paulie, used less and less time. Jaime also noticed Paulie became less participative as the project progressed.

When Jaime spoke with Paulie one-on-one, he asked him if what he had observed was really happening and why. Thankfully, Jaime had created a safe space within the team and Paulie explained what was going on. Paulie was the oldest member of the team by several years. He had been in the industry his entire career and brought a great deal of experience to the table. He did not grow up with a tablet in his lap and felt a little technologically outpaced by his teammates. English was also his second language, though he was quite fluent.

In the team's chat platform, Paulie noticed his posts were not getting the same response from Jaime as posts made by others, both in timeliness and thoroughness. Paulie admitted his posts were longer and more detailed than most, which was driven by the desire to demonstrate he was in command of the technology and the language. It was true, Jaime's responses to Paulie's posts were not as timely or thorough as the others. From Jaime's perspective, Paulie included so much detail that he did not need to add additional comments or follow up with questions. Paulie's ideas were also so well-developed, there was not much for Jaime to add. The delayed response in comparison to others was the result of Jaime saving Paulie's posts to the end of the day, or even the next morning, because of their length.

Jaime realized that while providing several channels for the team's voices to be heard was a catalyst for collaboration, each voice must be considered individually within each channel and "heard" with equal weight. How "equal weight" is defined can vary by channel. This is a new dimension of which leaders who desire to lead with an innovation mindset must be highly aware. Furthermore, Jaime's behavior in the channel played out in front of the others in chat, potentially sending subtle messages that could lead to unconscious biases towards Paulie and his comments. Over time, other team members began to wonder—if Jaime was singling out Paulie, could he single them out as well?

Fear and hesitation erode the collective feeling of psychological safety for the team and could lead to deteriorating communication and less collaboration, and consequently fewer effective solutions.

Benefits of Inclusive Leadership

➤ Employees divulge themselves in the innovative activities when they experience a quality relationship with leaders.

➤ The quality [of the] relationship between leader and employees motivates employees to independently take risks through, not only generating new ideas, but also promoting and implementing new ideas. This risk-taking motivation on the part of employees come [sic] when they perceive Psychological Safety (PS), that is, their environment is safe for interpersonal risk-taking.

➤ Extant research suggests that psychological safety motivates employees toward creative process engagement—to the extent to which employees engage in the problem-identification, information-searching, and ideas generation activities. *Zhang & Bartol, 2010* Zhou and Pan (2015) demonstrated that creative process engagement mediates [facilitates] the relationship between psychological safety and creativity.[9]

REDEFINING TWO ESSENTIAL TRADITIONAL LEADERSHIP CHARACTERISTICS

Creating a culture ready for innovation begins with you, the leader. It will not happen from the bottom up. Most companies are simply not wired that way. The culture of your company may be strong overall, but to become an innovation organization there will most certainly be some leadership behaviors within your organization that need to evolve. There are two traditional characteristics of leadership that are the cornerstones of this evolution: Humility and Trust.

Humility

Confucius said, "Humility is the solid foundation of all virtues." "The reward for humility and fear of the LORD is riches and honor and life." (*Proverbs 22:4*).

"Do nothing out of selfish ambition or vain conceit. Rather, in humility value others above yourselves, not looking to your own interests but each of you to the interest of the others." (*Philippians 2:3-4*)

You have probably read books and articles about it in modern contexts as it applies specifically to business. Level 5 leadership is a concept developed in the book *Good to Great* by Jim Collins. It crystallizes what Humility in leadership means today.[10] "Level 5 leaders display a powerful mixture of personal humility and indomitable will. They're incredibly ambitious, but their ambition is first and foremost for the cause, for the organization and its purpose, not themselves."

In leading with an innovation mindset, Humility takes on a slight, yet significant enhancement—adding a meaningful new twist to its traditional definition. Humility in the context of building a culture of innovation means **allowing others to influence your thinking**.

Sounds simple enough right? It's not. This is one of the most common psychological obstacles that stand between leading as you do today and becoming a leader with an innovation mindset. Consider your own professional journey and where it has led you today. Chances are you have progressed in your career not because of someone else's ideas, but because you were your own idea generator. You received recognition and credit for your own ideas early on and that continued to fuel the belief that you had to be the "idea generator." The notion is exacerbated in many organizations by the expectation that you and you alone should articulate a unique and inspiring vision, then enlighten your staff with the idea *you* came up with because you, after all, are the leader.

Leading with an innovation mindset requires that you free yourself from believing you must be responsible for all ideas. This new way of leading innovation empowers your team or department to collectively contribute to idea generation and to influence your thinking.

Why is this so critically important? Here's the deal. You are good at what you do, or you would not be where you are. You may even consider yourself an expert, which you likely are. Now consider this, the more expertise we possess in a specific field, the more rigid our mental network becomes. Rigid networks contribute to our inability to recognize breakthrough solutions. Expertise restricts our ability to ask the types of curious questions that will help uncover transformational ideas. Over time, we become so familiar with our subject matter that we lose the ability to break free of our baked-in contexts of how our work is to be done. The walls of our box of expertise are too high and thick to think our way out of. We are no longer able to view our work from new and different perspectives.

As an expert, like it or not, you are the least qualified person to come up with innovative ideas. The solution? Allow others to influence your thinking!

Good news: You're an expert in your field. Bad news: You're an expert in your field. Lose the expertise, gain the wisdom.

When you begin to allow others to influence your thinking, who you elect as the "others" becomes exceedingly important. Think of this group as your innovation council of counselors. Often the notion of counselors conjures images of mature, seasoned individuals who have already traveled down the road you are on and can help you avoid pitfalls, obstacles, and other dangers. This type of experienced counselor is valuable if we are talking about life, but not so much when we are talking about innovation.

> **CONSIDER THIS:** *Innovation peaks among innovators between 46 and 50 years of age.*[11]

This finding should influence who is on your innovation council of counselors—it should include younger people. This notion likely challenges long-held views of who you would traditionally elect to be on your wise council. It requires a great deal of Humility to pursue the guidance of younger, less experienced people and to truly hear and use their ideas over your own in a genuinely inclusive, psychologically safe setting.[12]

But wait, there is more! Gender. While increasing diversity in general increases performance, there is evidence that women have a major impact. In one wide-ranging study in which researchers at MIT and Carnegie Mellon sought to identify a general intelligence score for teams, they not only found that teams that included women achieved better results, but that the higher the proportion of women was, the better the teams did. If you are male and your innovation council consists of only male voices, you are missing an important perspective that only female minds can bring to an issue or opportunity.[13]

CONSIDER THIS: According to McKinsey & Company's 2018 Delivering Through Diversity *report, "Companies in the top quartile for gender diversity on executive teams were 21 percent more likely to outperform on profitability and 27 percent more likely to have superior value creation. The highest-performing companies on both profitability and diversity had more women in line (i.e., typically revenue-generating) roles than in staff roles on their executive teams."*

It is not only about gender. Companies in the top quartile for ethnic/cultural diversity on executive teams were 33 percent more likely to have industry-leading profitability. "That this relationship continues to be strong suggests inclusion of highly diverse individuals—and the myriad ways in which diversity exists beyond gender…can be a key differentiator among companies." Inclusion is an enabler of better thinking and better results. Note that inclusion does not merely mean that each seat at the table is filled with someone different than the next. It must be true that the voices from each seat are heard with impartiality and equal interest regardless of how audacious their ideas are or how their thoughts are presented. If your organization is to become an innovation organization, then allowing others to influence one's thinking is a behavior that must be modeled by **you**, the leader.[14]

Remember, we are talking about innovation. If your company needs to answer: "Are we doing the right things?" and "Are we doing things right?" then engage your innovation council. If it is facing change, engage your innovation council. If you are creating plans for next year, engage your innovation council. If there are problems that need to be overcome, engage your innovation council. In other words, if you want to create an innovation organization, redefine the role Humility plays in your leadership philosophy, surround yourself with diverse people who will exceed your expectations when it comes to diverse thinking, and make the practice of allowing others to influence your thinking come to life through your behavior.

This twist on Humility is contagious! If you are truly committed to it, it will be noticed and practiced by others in the organization. You should hold every leader accountable to do so. Doing so can only strengthen the culture of innovation.

> *"'Humble inquiry' is the fine art of drawing someone out, of asking questions to which you do not already know the answer, of building a relationship based on curiosity and interest in the other person."*
>
> —EDGAR H. SCHEIN

Trust

The "others" whom you should allow to influence your thinking beyond your innovation council of counselors should include your team. Regardless of years of experience, each of your team members is inherently wired to be a creative problem solver. Creating the right environment that unleashes breakthrough, innovative solutions begins with instilling trust among your entire team. This trust creates a safe and inclusive setting for idea sharing and solution finding. Trust, therefore, becomes a pivotal part of leading with an innovation mindset.[15]

> *TRUST: "Learning to trust is one of life's most difficult tasks."*
> *—Isaac Watts*

In its 2016 global CEO survey, PwC reported 55 percent of CEOs think that a lack of trust is a threat to their organization's growth.

Like humility, Trust is not a foreign concept. You are aware of the importance of establishing Trust as a leader. Doing what you say you will do and creating safe spaces for your team to be vulnerable are examples of traditional Trust constructs I'm sure you recognize. However, in the context of leading with an innovation mindset, Trust takes on a slightly different meaning than the traditionally held import.

Trust is at an all-time low. Research shows that interpersonal trust continues to decline. The percentage of people who believe "most people can be trusted" fell from 46 percent in 1972 to nearly 30 percent in 2014. We should expect the trending decline to continue. What impact might this have on your organization? In 2014, chances were that one out of every three people you hired did not trust you or each other. Projecting the trend farther into the future, it will be even fewer than that.

The value of allowing others to influence your thinking was established in our discussion of Humility. Think of Trust as an extension of that idea. Humility cannot exist without Trust, and Trust has no reason to exist outside of Humility. Trust, in the context of building a culture of innovation, suggests that you are handing over to others the responsibility to creatively solve problems of all kinds. You trust the people around you to leverage the innovation process properly and to experiment within its framework. You trust them to be curious, inquisitive, and thought-provoking. Like Humility, Trust behaviors must be modeled if they are to be adopted by the organization.

INTERPERSONAL TRUST
(UNITED STATES)

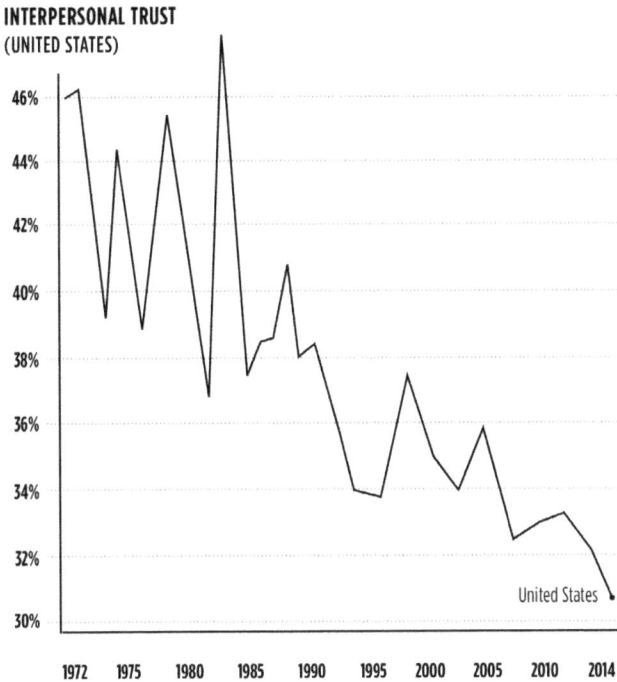

Source: US General Social Survey (2016)

Within the context of a culture of innovation, Trust is defined as your pledge to consistently model a set of specific behaviors.[16]

Hear new ideas with a curious ear and respond with interesting questions

My team can trust me to treat their ideas with honor, dignity, and respect in a place where they feel safe to share. Every time you can respond to an idea from anyone in your organization, you have the opportunity to demonstrate your commitment to transforming your culture into an innovation culture. Your response is evidence of your commitment. Leading an innovation organization with an innovation mindset requires that you reliably respond to ideas with only one thing—questions. Nothing communicates Trust like inquisitive probing about something, whether we are interested in it deep down or not. Even if you believe the idea may not be a strong one or is off strategy, asking questions about it usually leads the presenter of such ideas to either validate your assumptions or to disprove them, thus expanding your own innovative mindset.

The key difference in responding with questions instead of statements is that the person with the idea self-evaluates the quality of their idea through your questions. They arrive at the appropriate conclusion on their own instead of being told by you that their idea is strong or weak. They learn through experience and gain under-standing of the characteristics of a high-quality idea by thinking through your questions and formulating appropriate answers.

Responding to ideas with questions instead of statements pays two huge dividends. First, more staff will be inspired to think about ways to improve their work and present ideas originating from their individual perspective. Imagine having your entire staff thinking about solving problems and seizing opportunities right where they are, instead of a select few, or worse, you alone. The result will be a greater number of ideas. The more ideas that may solve a particular problem, the higher the likelihood of finding one that ends up being a game changer. Second, the quality of ideas from staff will increase significantly.

They know you will interrogate them about their ideas by asking questions such as:

➤ What problem does this actually solve?

➤ Is this problem a symptom or do you know the root cause of the problem you have identified?

➤ Whose problem is this?

➤ How long has this problem been going on?

➤ Why has it not been solved already?

➤ What/who inspired this idea?

➤ What needs to be true about this idea for it to be a success?

➤ Who did you talk to or collaborate with to help refine this idea?

➤ What resources will be needed to launch this idea?

➤ How has this idea changed between the time you first thought of it and today?

➤ What other ideas did you consider but rejected and why?

➤ What would cause this idea to fail?

➤ Who would be on the team that could develop this idea further?

➤ In what ways can this idea be bigger, ground-breaking, or transformational?

➤ What conditions would make this idea fail?

Over time, your staff and your leaders will present higher-quality ideas because your questions will become their questions and they will more thoroughly assess their ideas before they engage in a conversation about them with you. The time invested in this one attribute of leading with an innovation mindset could pay big dividends.

Protect the sharing of ALL ideas and the people who share them

There will be no future repercussions to a team member's reputation or career for sharing wild, outlandish, or opposing ideas. One of the biggest reasons why people who are new in their careers do not bother thinking about new and different ideas is the stigma that we have manufactured around ideas that are too far "out of the box." Consequently, they might miss the chance to contribute an idea that could ignite transformation within their organization. The possibility that sharing one crazy idea might brand them for the rest of their career as a loose, undisciplined maverick will keep them from pursuing ideas that are off the map. Yet those are the types of ideas that push us to seek new, better, bigger destinations and result in breakthrough innovations. Remember, younger people tend to possess greater ability for developing transformative ideas. Their ability to think freely (within a framework) about big ideas (that provide business value) is the fuel that powers the future of your organization. Celebrate the outlandish nature of wild thinking. Remember too, that if you are open to hearing all ideas, without judgment, the ideas you hear may be wild, but they will exist within a framework of solid thinking.

> *"Trust has positive and statistically significant correlation with the probability of becoming an entrepreneur. Trust leads to entrepreneurship, rather than the other way around."*

Establish Idea Equity

I will always welcome analysis and feedback of my own ideas and acknowledge that once my ideas are spoken, they are no longer mine alone. They are to be evaluated with the same weight as all the other ideas from everyone else. One of the most difficult things we can do as leaders is relinquish ownership of our ideas. Remember, it is the voice of traditional leadership behavior that tells us we must be the sole originators of ideas. People who lead with an innovation mindset know this is not true. An innovation leader believes in the power of 'we over me.' What would make you think your ideas are better than everyone else's? (*Reread the part about humility and being the expert.*). Your ideas are likely not as good as others, and there's a reason why.

The Innovator's DNA introduces two essential concepts: Discovery skills and Delivery skills. What should be a balanced relationship between the two views is frequently unbalanced in favor of Delivery.

➤ **Discovery Skills:** "The innovation skills of questioning, observing, networking, and experimenting constitute what we call the innovator's DNA, or code for generating innovative ideas." These skills are found frequently in founding entrepreneurs and fuel forwarding-looking ideas. Unfortunately, over time (a very short time in some cases), the amount of work and the incessant challenges of maintaining the day-to-day operation of your organization demands that you exercise more Delivery skills than Discovery skills.

➤ **Delivery skills**: "Analyzing, planning, detail-oriented implementing, and disciplined executing…critical for delivering
results." You will likely find yourself so caught up in managing the present that you are unable to imagine innovative
futures for your organization. There is no discovery going
on. You are so busy living in the world of "what is" that
you do not spend any time in the realm of "what if." The
result of that thinking is that your ideas are probably not
as great as you think they are. When your team tells you as
much, your response should be one of gratitude and appreciation for their honesty. They need to trust that you will
receive their constructive criticism with grace and sincere
appreciation.[12]

Trust the Innovation Process

Even though as the leader I have the authority to do so, I will not
circumvent the steps of the innovation process. I will model what
trusting the process looks like. Any practicing innovator will tell
you "trust the process!" The design thinking process has worked
for thousands of years. It always has, and it always will, but I
have seen many leaders compromise, water down, or altogether
ignore the stages of the innovation process. This disregard is due
to several reasons.

First, many leaders have a proclivity for action. They want to
see things happen. For that reason, they have a tendency to ignore
the Discover phase and begin with Design, then rush into Deploy—
or go straight to Deploy. (We will discuss the Discover-Design-
Deploy process in detail in a later chapter.) Another reason process

steps are ignored is due to unrealistic expectations in deploying an idea. Personal ego can get in the way and push leaders to avoid prototyping or testing because they do not want the unexpected outcomes to reflect negatively on their reputation as a leader.

Do any of these scenarios describe you at times? If so, you are not alone. But if you desire to create an innovation organization, you must demonstrate to your team that following the process matters a great deal to you. You must overcome any temptation to compromise the process and show the organization that you will not exit one stage of the process and go to the next one until every aspect of that stage has been fully explored and the outcome validated. If others see you cutting corners, they will feel enabled to do the same and innovation will not take hold at your organization.

Trust allows difficult and challenging conversations about the status quo, new directions, strategy, and vision to take place in healthy ways. What doesn't challenge us doesn't change us.

ONE MORE THING ON PEOPLE

Here are a few more tips to make the second P of Essential Innovation highly effective.

> ➤ Name a person to be responsible for innovation. This person and their team are not the chief innovators, but they will teach, coach, and consult people on the innovation process, guide project owners through it, and show how others can participate, lead, and teach the process. The innovation team does not own innovation. They own the responsibility of nurturing a *culture of innovation* and help create an army of vibrant everyday innovators.

➤ Assess your innovation hiring profile. Do you have one? Understanding a candidate's thinking style before they are hired helps to diversify the tribe.

➤ Create a bench of thinkers outside the organization, perhaps outside your industry, to offer an unbiased, naïve-expert perspective.

➤ Nurture an army of everyday innovators by embedding innovation coaches in every department throughout the organization.

➤ Co-create! Co-create! Customer-centric organizations are more innovative. Involve your end users in the innovation process.

An organization does not become an innovation organization by simply creating an innovation process. Leadership must be intentional about creating an innovation culture and lay a foundation of Humility. Humility leads to Trust. Trust leads to bold, wild, fantastic conversations in safe environments where new ideas can flourish. These conversations lead to vibrant, open, and effective collaboration. Only a culture where the **people** relate with one another in a sustainable, inclusive environment of collaboration at all levels and starting with the top, is ready for innovation.

William Johnsen said, "If it is to be, it is up to me." It is difficult but possible to create a culture of innovation. It requires a champion whose pioneering spirit can change the course of an organization in dramatic ways.

Who is this innovation champion in your organization? If it's not you, why not? The behaviors that were discussed in this chapter can be practiced tomorrow! You can lead by example and create an innovation culture that is absent of ego and rich with Humility and Trust, so collaboration can flourish and so can its people.

YOUR MOVE

REFLECTION:

What would my team say my question-to-statement ratio is? How would others describe how I treat their ideas? How would my team describe how well I invite their critique of my ideas? How would they describe how well I receive their opinion about my ideas?

REACTION:

What specific behaviors of Trust and Humility do I need to improve?

ACTION:

Self—To become a better leader with an innovation mindset, what will I do differently first, starting when?

Organization—Who will own the responsibility for transforming our organization into an innovation organization and what makes this person the best choice?

3

PHILOSOPHY

The third P of *Essential Innovation*, **Philosophy**, is a critical next step in creating a culture of innovation before moving into the process Ps four, five, and six. Taking this step assumes you have already adopted the second step, **People** behaviors, because there are essential questions that must be answered about the culture of innovation before innovation as a capability can be activated.

Many organizations wrestle at length with the Philosophy step. The work can be difficult, but the outcome is of utmost importance because it sets the trajectory for everything else that follows. Plan on lengthy discussions about what can seem like minutia, such as which word belongs where in the "we believe" statement about innovation. It is not minutia! Words matter. As we will discuss in this chapter, choosing the right words is critical for aligning everyone behind building an innovation organization. Whether or not innovation happens at your organization is determined by the Philosophy step outcomes, and the innovation legacy you and your leadership team will leave to your organization depends on it.

In this chapter, we will discuss each of these categories from an innovation perspective. You will be prompted to address the following questions:

➤ How do we want to become an innovation organization?

➤ What must we believe about ourselves and our company to become an innovation organization?

➤ When we become an innovation organization, what will be true about how innovation comes to life across our company?

➤ How will we equip staff with the tools to apply innovation methods to their work?

➤ What will be our common language of innovation that will become an ordinary part of our meetings, hallway chats, emails, presentations, etc.?

➤ When we become an innovation organization, how will the value of our work be measured?

➤ How will we hold staff accountable for our innovation behaviors?

The outcome of this chapter will be a framework that represents clearly defined building blocks for establishing the practice of innovation at your company. The steps you'll take are intended to provide guidance and direction. I encourage you to think about how to adapt this material in ways that are best suited for your specific organization.

Let us begin by defining what we mean by Philosophy. Philosophy is the study of fundamental questions concerning:

➤ Reason
➤ Beliefs
➤ Mind
➤ Knowledge
➤ Language
➤ Value

We will look at each of these through the lens of creating a culture of innovation. Each of the six philosophy elements should be approached with a great deal of thought while remembering that they are links of a culture chain, and that chain will only be as strong as its weakest link. With that said, let's begin.

REASON

Making sense of things
and practices.

FORMING THE INNOVATION PURPOSE STATEMENT

Your Innovation Purpose Statement explains the reason innovation exists at your organization. It will play a key role in launching the practice of innovation across your entire organization. It will help everyone make sense of why innovation is important to the growth of your company. Consider the Innovation Purpose Statement in three sections:

1. Long-term value or impact
2. An emotional connection
3. A catalyst for new areas of growth

Let's look at each one in order.

Long-term value / impact should answer questions about the difference that becoming an innovation organization will make over several years. Discuss who you are as an organization today and who you want to be in the future. Think big... really big. Where can becoming an innovation organization take you? Out of these discussions will come an increasingly clear purpose that innovation will play in that journey.

Suggested Long-term Value/Impact Questions

➤ How will our company be different in five years because we have become an innovation organization?

- What are things that will be true if nothing changes?

- What are things that will be true if we become an innovation organization? (This could include structuring the company to be as nimble and flexible as possible, having as few rigid systems as possible.)

➤ What do we want to be known for, and by whom do we want to be known?

- Be known for more than, "we are the most innovative company in our industry." Be specific. One natural water restoration company specialized in cleaning up oil spills in large bodies of water. It could have remained great within that niche but by becoming an innovation organization, it wanted to be known for its innovations in chemistry that restores damaged water-based ecosystems around the world. This expanded vision led to new markets that included water treatment in natural habitats damaged by disasters and reclaiming affected regions in extreme northern and southern regions due to climate change.

➤ What will be the evidence that we have become an innovation organization as seen by the people and communities we serve and by our staff?

- What do you want these audiences to say about you? What do they say now?

➤ What will be the tangible impact of our innovation organization on the world around us and globally?

- The company that specialized in oil spills might be able to see a thriving wildlife community or fewer hospitalizations due to water-borne illnesses post disasters.

Organization leaders must be careful not to merely state their vision, but to test their vision by running it through the innovation process. More on that in the next chapter.

I cannot overstate the importance of establishing an *emotional connection* with staff through the Innovation Purpose Statement. In fact, it is perhaps the most challenging aspect of any purpose statement. A meaningful connection between the Innovation Purpose Statement and what staff members do every day helps ensure that your Innovation Purpose Statement becomes a meaningful, living idea and not a corporate prop that hangs on a few walls around the office. The Innovation Purpose Statement is intended to be cited regularly, such as at the beginning of every project team, department and staff meeting, at leadership meetings, and so on. Infusing it with emotional connectivity will help ensure that it resonates with staff from now on.

Suggested Emotional Connection Questions

> ➤ Why should staff care that we are an innovation organization?

> - How does being an innovation organization give employees more meaning in their work?

> - In what ways will staff benefit from being part of an innovation organization?

> - What are the adjectives that we want employees to use in five years to describe our company? How do they describe it today?

> ➤ How do our customers and the people within the communities we serve currently describe our company? How do we want them to describe it in five years?

> ➤ How will our staff be different from employees of other organizations?

> How will our customers be changed for having done business with our company?

> How will our partners be different when we are an innovation organization?

- In what ways will staff feel connected to innovation?

- How can we make it personal for them?

- How can we create a naming convention for innovation projects that create an emotional connection to the work among the team?

Giving staff the permission and inspiration to create something much bigger than themselves becomes the catalyst for new areas of growth. This part of the Innovation Purpose Statement casts a vision for not only out-of-the-box thinking, but "unboxed" thinking. Unboxed thinking opens possibilities beyond the current context with which staff operate every day.

An Account Analyst should feel like they are just as empowered to approach their job as innovatively as the Head of Product Development does. Continuous improvement innovations are essential, but when staff can visualize their contributions to groundbreaking innovations, beyond what they believe is possible today, it can make the difference between mere continuous improvements and transformational innovations.

Suggested Catalysts for New Areas of Growth Questions

> What new and unexpected ways will we serve our customers and communities beyond the current core operations of our organization?

➤ What new customers and communities will we be able to serve innovatively?

➤ How does innovation fuel the long-term vision of our organization overall?

➤ In what ways will employees be supported in their efforts to think like futurists?

➤ How will employees be encouraged to try new things and how will they be recognized for their efforts?

BELIEFS

Rationale for believing what
the organization thinks
is or should be true.

FORMING "WE BELIEVE" STATEMENTS

A "We Believe" statement is like the core values of your organization—it articulates what your organization believes about work, customers, staff, the community, the environment, fairness, diversity and inclusion, care, etc. These values help explain where your company stands philosophically regarding essential topics.

The same approach is taken with the "We Believe" statement of innovation. When questions arise about any aspect of innovation, from people to process to projects to priorities to performance and so on, the "We Believe" statement should be something that any leader at any time can turn to for guidance.

The statement addresses specific points that must exist and must be true for innovation to exist and flourish within your organization. These points can be related to expectations for leadership roles, conditions under which innovation can thrive, conditions that must be avoided, rationale for why innovation as a capability is important, how risk is assessed, alignment on how to view innovation relative to other departments, and justification for innovation that falls within reason and connects to the organization's existing business strategy. Write your "We Believe" statement in a fashion that suggests innovation will blend into the organization, accentuating its positives and leveraging its core competencies, not a bolt-on sidecar of activities unrelated to what the company is all about.

The "we" in the "We Believe" statements include everyone in the organization. That means the statement is not only for the innovation group's consumption; rather it is for the entire organization. It is not something believed only by those tapped with "doing innovation," nor is supporting it a condition to do innovation. That is not to say everyone must agree with or believe it, but there should be something in the statement that anyone in the organization can read and think, "Yeah, that makes sense to me." Let's look at three examples.

WE BELIEVE	We Believe everyone has a voice and is responsible for thinking innovatively.	We Believe our work requires an innovation mindset with a future-forward perspective.	We Believe there is an optimal balance of strategy and curiosity.
BELIEF ACTIVATED	All staff are accountable for their roles as innovators first and functional contributors second. Everyone is obligated to think innovatively in every position in our company.	Establishing new streams of opportunities by creating new service models should be driven by a deliberate pursuit of off-the-map opportunities without losing sight of where we started.	Forging a variety of new "futures" should be done within a sound framework of operating principles and the innovation process. We must trust the process we create.

Not all "We Believe" statements look alike. Some organizations will have one statement that makes one point, one statement that includes several points, or several statements that make several points. Make it simple to read and digest. Overcomplicating it will only create ambiguity and that may trip up your staff when questions about innovation and its practice at your organization arise... and they will surely arise.

MIND

Relating to the body. The innovation team: who we are.

FORMING THE INNOVATION TEAM'S PURPOSE, ROLES, AND NORMS

The **Mind** component of Philosophy is a double-click on the Purpose and "We Believe" statements. It explains how the innovation team defines itself and its role(s), and how it relates to the rest of the corporate body. Recall from the previous chapter that the innovation team is the group of people who are ultimately responsible for innovation at your organization, but they do not "own" innovation! The innovation team teaches, coaches, consults, encourages employees to use the innovation process, guides project owners through it, and shows how others can participate in and even teach it to other staff.

Think of the innovation team as its own unit with its own personality, characteristics, and expectations for how someone from this innovation team behaves. You may be asking why the innovation team would behave differently than everyone else on staff. The answer has to do with perspective. They must be protected from the gravitational pull of the core operation so they have the time and space to think and try things that the people who are managing the core business simply cannot do. Also, the innovation team should not be evaluated using the same performance metrics as the rest of the staff.

That performance measurement component is why the Philosophy step is so important. The innovation team is a unit that empowers, equips, and inspires others to think innovatively and to do innovation well.

Consider this: historically, companies have largely hired "doers." The staff at most organizations represents people who get things done. They are usually over-burdened and under-resourced and have more to do than either time or money will realistically allow them to accomplish. They are heads-down, focused on supporting the week-to-week operations of their department. If managing core operations consumes all the oxygen in your organization, innovation will suffocate and die. Therefore, you must intentionally carve out unique roles for a team that has enough fresh air to think about how to create and grow an innovation organization.

In some cases, the innovation "team" may consist of only one person. That is okay! The same philosophy applies to them. It may even be a part-time role at first, but leadership must vigorously protect the time this role spends on innovation and be a proponent for growing the capability into a full-time position. Ultimately this single person role should evolve into a team of people, if that is what is required.

The roles and responsibilities of the innovation team should also be clearly defined in a "Who We Are" statement. For example, a retail company divides the work of its innovation team into four categories: Consultant, Facilitator, Educator, and Simulations.

➤ **Consultant |** This role helps teams understand how to apply the innovation process. Sometimes teams start down the innovation path without having accomplished the planning work upfront that helps ensure a successful project. Other times a team can become stuck in a particular stage of the innovation process and needs help getting unstuck. This role can identify blind spots team leaders do not see.

➤ **Facilitator |** This role designs and facilitates innovation sessions and workshops that help teams move through the innovation process as efficiently as possible. This role works with team leaders to plan sessions that are aimed to achieve a specific goal, which is often determined with the help of a consultant who is skilled in the appropriate technologies for virtual sessions or who has a partner who can act as the session producer. Facilitated sessions are more effective than when the team leader leads them because a skilled facilitator can move the conversations along and keep them on point, press the group to dig deeper when appropriate, and surface necessary topics that the lead may feel uncomfortable raising.

➤ **Educator |** This role equips employees to think like innovators and enables them to create innovations using the innovation process. An educator designs curriculum and learning modules to be consumed by employees. The educator also creates and hosts innovation-based, culture-building events such as Lunch & Learns, speaker series, and workshops. Communication is key for this role. There should always be inspiring stories and compelling information coming from the innovation team to the entire organization.

➤ **Simulation Leader |** Rapid prototyping requires resources that can build a prototype and conduct multiple simulations with it. This could be a team of programmers, skilled fabricators, or both. The simulation lead role can be in-house or outsourced. The retail company referenced above uses on-site designers and fabricators with an on-site workshop to build anything from sketches of an idea, to small-scale modeling, to life-size construction, to virtual reality. Whatever level of definition is needed to run effective simulations, this team can do it.

Having these four roles clearly mapped out and defined make it clear how the innovation team serves the greater organization. Doing so also provides everyone in the organization with clarity about how they can interact with the innovation team and what services the team can offer them.

CENTRALIZED OR DECENTRALIZED INNOVATION MODEL

Here we will explain the differences between a centralized and a decentralized model of innovation. As mentioned earlier, someone must be responsible for creating an innovation organization. Make no mistake, this dedicated person or team is essential whether centralized or decentralized is the preferred model. Practically, the distinction between the two models is in how innovation and ideas flow within and around the organization. Philosophically, the differences between the two models are vast and significant. Let us look at the pros and cons of each model.

CENTRALIZED	DECENTRALIZED
ALL innovation begins, is managed by, and is launched from the innovation team only.	Innovation is the responsibility of everyone in the organization.
PROS	**PROS**
Better ensures that the process of innovation is maintained and applied properly.	Collaboration is significantly wider and can occur more often.
Can explore a wider variety of options faster due to its separation from the core organization.	Ideas are more likely to be adopted because the people closest to the work are part of the ideation.
The innovation process can be expedited by the subject matter expertise of the innovation team through consistently executing the innovation process.	Creates an army of everyday innovators, potentially leading to bigger breakthrough ideas at all levels of the organization.
CONS	**CONS**
Sometimes gaining support for unique ideas is difficult as they are handed off to another team to launch and support.	Equipping and educating the greater organization is an ongoing and time-consuming responsibility of the innovation team.
Breakthrough ideas may not surface from the greater organization because there is a "not my job" mentality.	Creating interest in the consistent practice of the innovation process can be challenging when budgets are tight. Innovation is typically the first thing to go when times are tough.
Time and effort can be consumed exploring innovations that may not align with organizational priorities.	The innovation process can become diluted over time as practitioners make subtle changes to the process to suit their specific needs.

The model that is best for your organization may largely depend on how it is organized. For example, if your management structure is more hierarchical with vertical levels of management and few decision makers, a Centralized model may be the best fit. If your management structure is flatter, less hierarchical and decision rights are distributed throughout the organization, a Decentralized model may work best.

I encourage you to consider the Decentralized model first. It is the model that contributes the most culturally to an innovation organization. One key differentiation of the Decentralized model is the opportunity for everyone (beginning with the department leaders) to use the innovation process to better deal with changes and disruptions that will surely come their way. Remember, being prepared and leading through change and handling disruption well are the key reasons for creating an innovation organization in the first place. Decentralizing the application of innovation across the entire organization, under the guidance and coaching of a dedicated innovation team, helps ensure everyone is prepared to flourish in times of change.

KNOWLEDGE

Awareness, comprehension,
recognition, and mastery.

FORMING THE INNOVATION PROCESS

It's important to begin the Innovation Process by determining the degree to which innovation becomes an integral part of ongoing training and education in your organization. Many organizations deal with this component as an afterthought and then find it difficult to gain buy-in and funding late in the process, when resources and support are needed most. If staff feel like they are ill-equipped to easily apply innovation processes to their work, they will avoid adopting innovation as a capability and prevent a culture of innovation from developing.

Even if you have someone responsible for staff learning and development, innovation training and education are different from how professional development is approached in general. There is a philosophical difference between general learning and development in a traditional organization and innovation learning and development in an innovation organization. Now in this early phase is the time to define what exactly the role of innovation training and development will play in your organization.

If your organization desires to become an innovation organization and to achieve meaningful innovative outcomes, then there are two areas of innovation your staff must comprehend:

➤ **Education**—awareness and understanding of innovation principles and process

➤ **Application**—effectively setting innovation principles and processes into practice

Education and Application are connected and work in a perpetual cycle. An organization cannot become an innovation organization without fully realizing the potential of its people to be the innovators they are capable of being. This potential is realized through both Education and Application training and development.

We will discuss innovation training and development in more detail and the importance of its ongoing nature in Chapter Six (*Permanence*). For now, you need to define the level of importance that innovation training and development will have relative to other activities within your organization. I encourage you to place innovation training and development on the same level of importance as your key business initiatives. Why? The degree to which your organization will successfully survive change is directly related to how well your people are prepared and able to lead with an innovation mindset. That only happens through ongoing, thoughtful, engaging, effective innovation Education and Application training and development.

LANGUAGE

Commonality and agreement.

FORMING A COMMON LANGUAGE

A common language is the foundation of every culture. Your organization is no different, and an innovation culture is especially dependent on a shared language. The process of innovation has many moving parts and without a common language binding these parts to the greater whole in consistent ways, the application of innovation principles and processes become diluted as everyone begins to do the work of innovation in increasingly disconnected and individualistic ways. It's common for people to adapt established processes to fit their personal style or approach. When we do, collaboration breaks down, great ideas cease to be discussed, and people eventually stop seeing the value in investing in innovation capabilities. When breakdown happens, the organization is no longer producing competitive innovations. We've seen this process happen with companies like Blockbuster and Kmart. The company ceases to be relevant. Growth slows, profits dwindle and ultimately, the company closes its doors for the last time.

A shared language can help form guardrails around innovation thinking and activities so that the integrity of the process is maintained long-term. The first step is to identify the words your organization will use in relation to innovation, beginning with how the word "innovation" is defined. (Note this is different from its purpose.) Defining innovation for your organization helps staff know how to refer to innovation in everyday conversations. The process might be as simple as leaning on the Merriam-Webster definition of innovation (1: a new idea, method, or device, 2: the introduction of something new). But if more detail or specificity is needed for your organization, you will need to refine how you describe various types of innovation.

GLOSSARY OF INNOVATION TERMS

It is important to assemble a glossary of terms that have to do with your company's culture, the capabilities of innovation, and your company's innovation process. Common language is the glue that binds thoughts and ideas together and makes the sharing of ideas frictionless. Your glossary might include the following. It is not uncommon for the glossary to continue to grow over time.

CULTURAL	CAPABILITIES
Inclusion	Innovation
Internal Collaboration	Process Steps
External Collaboration	Practitioner
Innovation Mindset	Gather
Trust	Examine
Humility Metrics	Ideation Prototype

Over 100 terms can be found at https://www.viima.com/innovation-glossary

THE TYPES OF INNOVATION MODEL

The model below suggests four types of innovation: Routine, Breakthrough, Disruptive and Transformative. Why is it important to make definition distinctions between the types of innovation? Being aware of which type of innovation you are doing provides opportunities to have discussions about how resources are allocated and where resource tradeoffs should and should not occur. Let's take a closer look at the Types of Innovation model below.

NEW
5

BREAKTHROUGH
Do brand-new things to make
the good things better

TRANSFORMATIONAL
Do brand-new things in
brand-new arenas

CAPABILITIES

A

2 | 4

1 | 3

B

ROUTINE
Do things to keep the
good things going

DISRUPTIVE
Take what we do best
in the new arenas

1

EXISTING
1

ORGANIZATIONAL MODEL

NEW
5

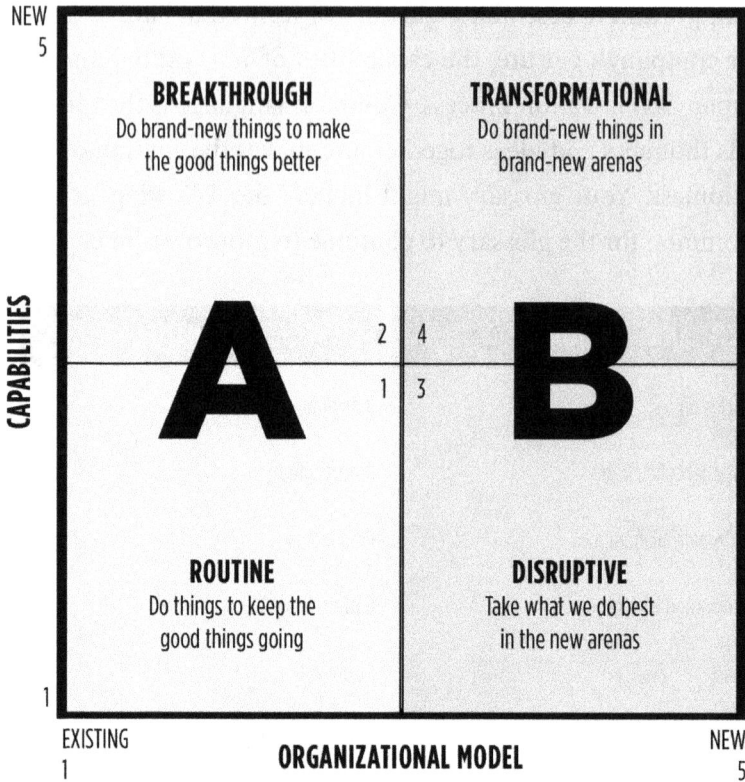

A — INNOVATIONS
Focus is on near-term
innovations that sustain growth
for the core organization.

B — INNOVATIONS
Focus is on foundations of
future growth based on the
2030 audience journey map.

Adapted from The Innovator's Dilemma[17]

The value of implementing an Innovation Definition Model like this one is that all the innovation work taking place can be visualized by plotting current projects among the four quadrants. Here's how it works.

Horizontal Axis

➤ **Step 1:** Write the name and a brief description on a project card or sticky note.

➤ **Step 2:** Score each project by the degree to which it requires that the organization makes some sort of change to complete the project with excellence. If a project can comfortably achieve its goal within the current organizational structure as is, without changing anything, then assign it a value of 1. If a project requires that a new sub-organization or entity or that certain resources be allocated differently, assign that project a value of 5.

➤ **Step 3:** Place the project card along the bottom of the horizontal axis according to its numeric value.

Vertical Axis

➤ **Step 4:** Score each project by the degree to which new capabilities are required to complete it. If the project does not require any new resources (e.g., new technology or highly skilled talent) then assign it a value of 1. If the project requires a significant investment in brand-new capabilities, assign it a value of 5.

➤ **Step 5:** Take each project card on the horizontal axis and move it vertically according to its capabilities score. (*Note: Move the project cards vertically like an elevator, making sure no two cards are in the same horizontal plane.*)

Interpreting the Results

At the end of the exercise, you will have a visual representation of the type of innovations that are currently at play, and each one should be acknowledged for the type of innovation it is. Not all innovation projects will be Transformational. Does Routine mean less important? Absolutely not! It simply means your organization is likely spending most of its time on continuous improvement projects. Routine innovation is critical for the ongoing health of the core business. Every project, regardless of its nature, should begin with fully understanding what the problem is exactly and whether it is the right problem to solve. The question is, how many innovation projects should fall into the **B** quadrants, if any?

At some point, you will be faced with either a change that is too complex to solve with A box innovations or an opportunity that can only be seized through B box innovations.

Defining the different types of innovations through establishing a common language makes it easier to recognize the moves that are (and are not) necessary to manage change and disruption successfully. Other opportunities to establish a common language include the steps of the innovation process you create. We will discuss the innovation process in the next chapter.

THE INNOVATION AREA CHART

Another way to view projects is by employing the Innovation Area Chart. Analyzing projects by how they employ capabilities and to what degree they change the business model brings clarity about where the bulk of the organization's resources are spent. While the balance can vary by industry, a common benchmark to consider is 70% of the projects are Routine, 20% are Breakthrough, and 10% are Transformational. The level of difficulty, amount of risk, and the amount of time the project will take increases from the Routine area to the Transformational area.

Take all the projects that make up your organization's annual budget and plot them on the Innovation Area Chart. You will quickly grasp what types of innovations in which your organization is investing.

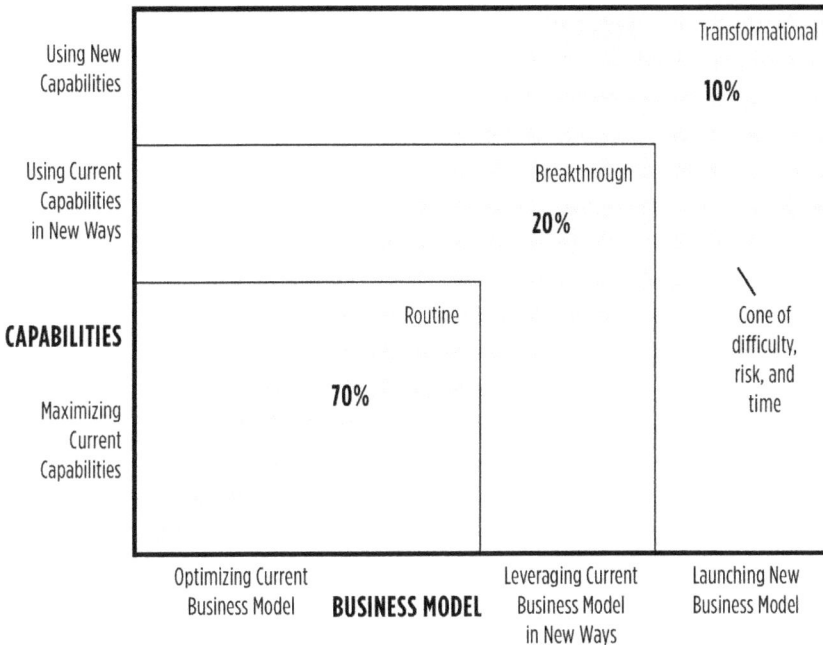

Adapted from McKinsey & Company's The Three Horizons of Growth[18]

VALUE

Assigning worth and
judging usefulness.

FORMING INNOVATION METRICS

Innovation is much more than brainstorming for ideas. It is an investment of time and energy that should be measured against other work on which the same time and energy might have been better spent. Assigning a value to innovation can be a challenging endeavor.

Suggested Questions for Measuring Non-Financial Innovation Performance

➤ What value should we place on solving a problem or seizing an opportunity?

➤ How do we measure the success of an idea?

➤ How do we measure how well we execute the innovation process? What are the merits of an idea's uniqueness and creativity? How well is the process executed?

➤ How sustainable is the innovation?

➤ How do we know when our staff is doing innovation well? How many staff are doing it? How quickly do they move through the process? What is their attitude towards it?

➤ How do we assess the quality of collaboration around our organization?

➤ How should we handle projects that do not meet expectations?

These questions are only a beginning!

Exercise a great deal of caution when discussing how innovation should be measured. Innovation is not like other functional areas within the core operations of a company. It is more than just what you do. It is also about how you think about what you do. Assessing the work of core operations can often be thought of in terms of **performance gaps**. How did the company do versus how it thought it would do? How can it reduce cost and waste while driving more efficiencies into its core processes? While some aspects of innovation can and should be measured in performance gap terms, many aspects of Disruptive and Transformational innovation should be considered in terms of **possibility gaps**.

Suggested Questions for Measuring Possibility Gap Value

➤ How accurately did we identify our most important audience?

➤ How well did we serve our most important audience by addressing their biggest need to be met, problem to be solved, or obstacle to overcome?

➤ What was the number of innovation projects that were launched this year? Is the number increasing or decreasing versus last year?

➤ What was the quality of each project's value to its audience?

➤ To what degree did projects demonstrate a vision of what is possible, beyond what is typically predictable?

➤ What was the stated evidence of excellence with each innovation project and to what degree did the evidence appear in the launched solution?

WHY METRICS MATTER

Beyond the stated value of Performance Gap and Possibility Gap measures, there are other benefits of measuring innovation, such as:

➤ Fostering Engagement

- People are not interested in watching a football game without a scoreboard. Metrics provide a reason to stay involved in the game and continue to work towards a stated goal. The right metrics create actions that are focused and clear.

➤ Establishing Direction

- People know they are on the right course when they are presented with values that demonstrate they are moving things in the right (or wrong) direction.

➤ Reducing Judgment

- Numbers do not lie. People are less likely to form subjective opinions about the value of a project when given valid quantifiable data. The performance of the team will speak for itself through such metrics whether or not there is agreement with the "likability" of the idea.

Characteristics of Innovation Metrics

As with any data used to measure business decisions, innovation metrics must have the following characteristics:

➤ **Quantifiable**–There is something about the value of every innovation that can be calculated, from new product sales and profit margins to efficiency gains in time, quality, or costs, to employee satisfaction and engagement, to name a few.

➤ **Verifiable**–The data must be valid and accurate, and the same formulas must be used consistently.

➤ **Understandable**– Make the information easy to access and consume.

- Include the baseline, trend line, and goal
- Provide a clear legend and defined units of measure
- Proactively provide explanations for commonly asked questions

MEASURING FAILURE

Another common metric attached to innovation is Failure Rate. For years, innovators have been trying to convince themselves and others that failure is a good thing. This concept has been previously discussed but bears repeating. Humans are hard-wired to avoid failure at all costs. Failing is bad. Not failing is good.

Rather than wasting time and energy attempting to convince staff that failing is a good thing, change the narrative. Speak in terms of unexpected outcomes and incorporate them into your common language.

The idea of unexpected outcomes is the positive opposite of failure's negative connotation.

Instead of trying to reduce failures to zero, we want to surface as many unexpected outcomes as possible. Unexpected outcomes discovered during prototyping points us to areas where the idea needs refinement. After initial refinements are made, we solicit audience feedback again and watch and listen for more unexpected outcomes. We continue to refine and iterate until there are no more unexpected outcomes. At that point, the idea has been refined as much as it can be and is ready to deploy. While the iterative process could elongate the project timeline, it should not be criticized because it is far better to deploy a successful idea late than to introduce an unsuccessful innovation on time.

No one wants to deploy any type of innovation that does not meet expectations. Discovering unexpected outcomes can reduce the chances of unmet potential. Measure each project by the number of unexpected outcomes discovered and recognize teams for how well they mined for them, even if it elongated the project timeline.

Defining the innovation philosophy at your organization can determine every aspect of its innovation culture. Innovation is not just something it does; it reflects who the company is at its soul. A fertile cultural soil of innovation must exist for the seeds of innovation to grow and produce fruit.

WHO will you be as an innovation organization?

HOW will your employees, vendors, competitors, and customers describe your innovativeness?

WHAT your organization believes about innovation will drive the quality of the behaviors which lead to consistently delivering successful innovations.

HOW innovation is structured within your organization determines how wide its influence may reach. If the goal is to become an innovation organization, the topics discussed in this chapter should be carefully understood and supported by everyone in the organization.

YOUR MOVE

REFLECTION:

To what degree am I willing and able to lead the transformation of our culture into an innovation culture? What am I most excited about? What am I most afraid of?

REACTION:

How long am I willing to give myself to make this transformation into an innovation organization happen?

ACTION:

What team of people should I assemble to create our innovation philosophy, and by when? Which senior leaders will support it? Which senior leaders will push back against it and why? How can objections be overcome?

4

PROCESS

In this chapter, we will present a **process** for making innovation happen in your organization. Before we discuss each step of the innovation process, we must address the importance of teaming. Without successfully aligning the project team prior to entering the innovation process, the outcome will likely take longer and will not deliver the value it could have had team alignment occurred first.

Alignment consists of several elements including shared purpose, norms (communication expectations, meeting attendance, conflict resolution, etc.), role clarity, decision rights, dependencies, timeframes, milestone deliverables, and so on. Teaming is an essential process within a process.

Recall the story of Jaime from Chapter Two. He was leading a project developing a new product for commercial kitchens. One afternoon, Jaime received a phone call from his boss. She said the leadership team had decided to pursue a new product development project and he had been tapped to lead it. She listed eight people who were to be included as part of this team. They had been selected because of the cross-functional nature of their roles and the contributions leadership believed they could bring to the project. It would be Jaime's decision whether to add additional members.

Jaime's first action was to bring this new team together for a kickoff meeting. In this initial meeting he asked the team what they believed the goal for the project was, what value they each brought to the project, what their role was as a team member, and who else should be included on the team. Each member struggled to answer the questions. When it came to who else should be included, the team came up with an additional eight people. Now the team was twice its size, and no one was clear on why they were there or what role they played. Working through the innovation process at this point would have a disastrous outcome.

This situation is more common than not. Many times, people are asked to lead projects that are defined by the deliverable only (the "what"), and not given guidance on the "how." It is up to the project leader to make sure that sufficient team alignment occurs to ensure that time is not wasted on chasing down answers to questions as the project progresses that should have been answered upfront. Projects become sources of frustration for the team and senior leaders when innovation and teams are fighting each other. Before jumping into the innovation process, take the time to do effective teaming basics.

NINE DIMENSIONS OF SUCCESSFUL TEAMING

1. **Purpose |** Successful teams start with a clear purpose and vision of success. Having a clear and agreed-upon mission helps define why the team exists and enables the creation and execution of strategies. When the whole team understands and agrees upon the purpose, they create a sense of shared meaning, and the team can make a more significant impact.

2. **Context |** To be successful, every team must understand the broader context of how they fit within the organization and where the need for the team is coming from. Teams need to understand the business challenge, the interdependencies they have with other groups, and what the customer wants. When teams understand how they fit into the larger picture, team members tend to be more invested in the outcome. They require less outside guidance and become more autonomous—proactively working to address problems and roadblocks instead of waiting for instructions.

3. **Structure |** Structure defines the talent, establishes roles and responsibilities, and outlines the decision-making process. The structure should describe the team leader's role, the responsibilities for each team member, and the team's degree of collaboration. Building structure around how decisions get made and how problems are solved are critical success factors for every team.

4. **People and Resources |** Understanding existing potential resources and talent is essential to implementing a team's purpose. Resources include time, equipment, supplies, information, budget, and most importantly, people. An inventory

of existing or needed skills, abilities, and expertise is an important ongoing part of successful team performance as goals change and evolve. When selecting new team members, look for people unlike yourself or others on your team to eliminate skills gaps and create new strengths. If every member of your team was great at the same things, there would be no one to handle the other stuff. Great teams have a diverse group of people, skill sets, and backgrounds. Diverse teams solve problems sooner because they bring a variety of ideas that enable them to choose the best solution faster.

5. **Planning** | Planning translates purpose into day-to-day actions, and the more complete the planning is, the less rework there will be. Creating specific and measurable work plans involves identifying tasks, sequencing those tasks in helpful ways, and assigning those tasks to team members with deliverable dates and check-in points.

6. **Morale** | Individual and team engagement and buy-in are critical underlying success factors that support a high-performing team's development. When team members have high morale, they are more committed, put in the effort required to overcome obstacles, and believe the team can be successful. Recognition of efforts and understanding of personal motivations by the team's leadership, understanding of the team's broader team context and purpose, and active participation in team activities drive strong team engagement.

7. **Operations** | Operations are the team processes and behaviors that enable highly functional team dynamics. These team processes include team meeting productivity, reward and recognition, learning and development, and

performance management. Establishing healthy team processes is essential for avoiding self-oriented behaviors like blaming, withdrawing, or competing against others. These operating principles establish the rules of engagement and build a continuous improvement mindset.

8. **Communication |** Establishing healthy and open communication processes is vital for a successful team. This includes ensuring meaningful dialogue, defining appropriate methods (email, text, phone), and frequently sharing information. Determining how to deliver feedback and resolve conflict is also an essential part of every team's communication processes, along with the appropriate times to collaborate.

9. **Results |** Every high-performing team focuses on achieving high-quality results. Great teams are clear about their results and how to measure the desired business and people outcomes. They effectively progress, demonstrate results to upper management, and strive for high degrees of excellence. [19]

The importance of getting teaming right cannot be overstated. The success of the project and whether a successful innovation deploys at all may depend on it. Build teaming into your project plan and allow ample time for clarifying conversations to emerge and for chasing down answers that eliminate ambiguities. Only healthy, high-performing teams do innovation well.

ORIGIN AND BENEFITS OF THE INNOVATION PROCESS

With a strong team formed and ready to apply its innovation process, let us first explore the nucleus of any innovation process: design thinking. The Interaction Design Foundation defines design thinking thusly:

> *"Design Thinking is a design methodology that provides a solution-based approach to solving problems. It's beneficial in tackling complex problems that are ill-defined or unknown, by understanding the human needs involved, by re-framing the problem in human-centric ways, by creating many ideas in brainstorming sessions, and by adopting a hands-on approach in prototyping and testing. The five stages of Design Thinking, according to the Hasso-Plattner Institute of Design at Stanford (d.school), are as follows: Empathize, Define (the problem), Ideate, Prototype, and Test."* [20]

It is important to acknowledge these foundation stages so that you can create an innovation process that best fits your organization while remaining true to the principles of design thinking. Some companies have additional stages such as Validate, Launch, and Live. Other companies may break down a certain stage into multiple substages. The point here is to not create an innovation process for your organization without incorporating the five principle stages of design thinking.

Innovation is commonly misunderstood to be a creative process. Although creative problem solving is part of it, the innovation process is a solidly strategic exercise. Two of the most important questions any leader of an organization should ask are: 1) Are we doing the right things? and 2) Are we doing things right? These are deeply strategic questions, and the innovation process answers them. As you read, think of the innovation process as a method for not only achieving specific project-level innovations, but also for short- and long-range strategic planning.

Among many, the chief benefits of the innovation process are that it provides clarity and focus. That's because at each stage of the innovation process, you must ask yourself whether you have sufficient clarity and adequate focus before moving on to the next stage. The natural tendency of many projects is to move away from the original scope of the work and morph into something slightly different that takes the work off target. The innovation process allows you to thwart potential drifts by providing a sure and credible reference point of understanding through in-depth knowledge about the audience for whom you are designing and their most important needs and opportunities.

Here's a typical example. As ideas are shared, particularly with senior leadership who like to add on to ideas, people will exert their own creative contributions and "we should also do this" and "wouldn't it be cool if…" suggestions. This situation introduces two problems. One, people tend to retain ownership of their ideas and to resist assigning their idea's destiny to others. Two, people, especially senior leaders, believe their ideas are good ones and should have a prominent place in the innovation discussion.

Having an innovation process allows you to measure the merits of add-on ideas based on how well they meet the criteria surfaced through and defined by the innovation process. Without an established innovation process, the merit of an add-on idea is simply a difference of opinion and the argument whether to incorporate the add-on idea is usually won by the person holding the highest title—inviting scope creep, confusion, and ambiguity.

While all ideas are welcome, they should all be measured against the unbiased insights that the innovation process generates. This lens helps prevent the innovation project from losing its clarity and focus and allows the process to work effectively and efficiently, unencumbered by less informed outside influences.

I asked 30 business professionals employed by large corporations across a variety of industries to describe their organization's innovation process. Half of them presented 15 different innovation processes. (The other half were unsure whether their company had a process or where to find it. We will tackle that issue in Chapter 6.)

At this point, you may be asking, "I thought innovation was a universal process?" You are right. While the process of doing innovation has design thinking aspects that should be present regardless of industry, it is flexible enough so that each organization can create its own version of the innovation process that best fits its business model and culture. The framework discussed in this chapter represents the basic components of the **process** of innovation, as well as the thinking styles and how to approach each stage. What it looks like at your organization is up to you.

The innovation process must be dutifully managed. One stage in the process cannot be disconnected from the rest. If that happens, the process falls apart and innovation ceases. Full effort and attention must be applied to each stage for the process to fully realize its value. What will be the criteria for moving from one stage to the next and who owns that decision are just a few of the key issues the project lead must manage. The innovation process works—it always has, and it always will. If a project is not successful, the cause will not be with the process, but rather how it was managed.

THINKING TYPES AND THE INNOVATION PROCESS

You will notice in my discussion of each stage I include the correlating thinking type. There are four different thinking types that correlate to each step of the innovation process: Investigator, Inventor, Investor, Implementer. It will be important to understand the thinking types of the project team to ensure that the team is not weighted toward any one particular thinking type.

Most of us are capable of thinking within any of the four thinking types at any given time. However, we are likely to have one thinking type that is dominant. If you had to choose to function within only one thinking type all day long, which one would leave you the most energy at the end of the day? That type is your dominant thinking type. Which thinking type are you?

Here are the characteristics of each one:

Investigators

- Have an insatiable curiosity energized by the need to "know"
- Were the kids who always asked "why"
- Go deep in understanding everything about that topic in which they are interested
- Enjoy working with structure and process because it yields better understanding
- Are empathetic explorers—wanting to know what it's like to "walk in their shoes"
- Highest energy stage: Discover

Inventors

- ➤ Have a curiosity that is driven by the fulfillment that comes from exploring

- ➤ Were the kids who always asked "why not"

- ➤ Often think of ways to make things they learn about or experience better

- ➤ Prefer working unstructured but excel when goals and guardrails are clear (root cause)

- ➤ Experience a sense of accomplishment when they combine unrelated things to make something new

- ➤ Highest energy stage: Design

Investors

- ➤ Are forward-thinking networkers

- ➤ Connect the dots and see relationships around concepts and ideas before others do

- ➤ Are often the voice of reality that identifies potential obstacles regarding new ideas

- ➤ Analyze situations and define a variety of potential consequences, both positive and negative

- ➤ Are more calculated decision makers who will often seek to involve others for their perspective

- ➤ Highest energy stage: Develop (also the evaluation of ideas in the back end of Design)

Implementers

- Are action-oriented
- Will do whatever it takes to achieve a goal because they don't like to fail
- Require just enough information to believe that what they are asked to accomplish is worth it
- Are detail-oriented with strong project management skills
- Are adaptable and able to make changes on the fly
- Highest energy stage: Deploy

It is essential to know the dominant thinking types of your team because certain thinking types at particular innovation stages add more value than other types. For example, Investigators thrive when they can get into the details of NPOs and discover root causes. That is a powerful asset in the Discover Stage. However, they can become bored with the creative process and disengage in the Design Stage.

Thinking type awareness is important because when you are working through the innovation process you can unintentionally demonstrate unhealthy behavior in sessions that do not excite your dominant thinking type. As long as you are aware of your tendencies and how you might be inclined to show up, you can adjust your mindset toward more productive behaviors. The most effective innovation teams are those consisting of a balance among the four thinking types. (For a detailed explanation of healthy and unhealthy behavior by thinking type, see the chart in the Appendix.)

This is a diagram of a generic innovation process:

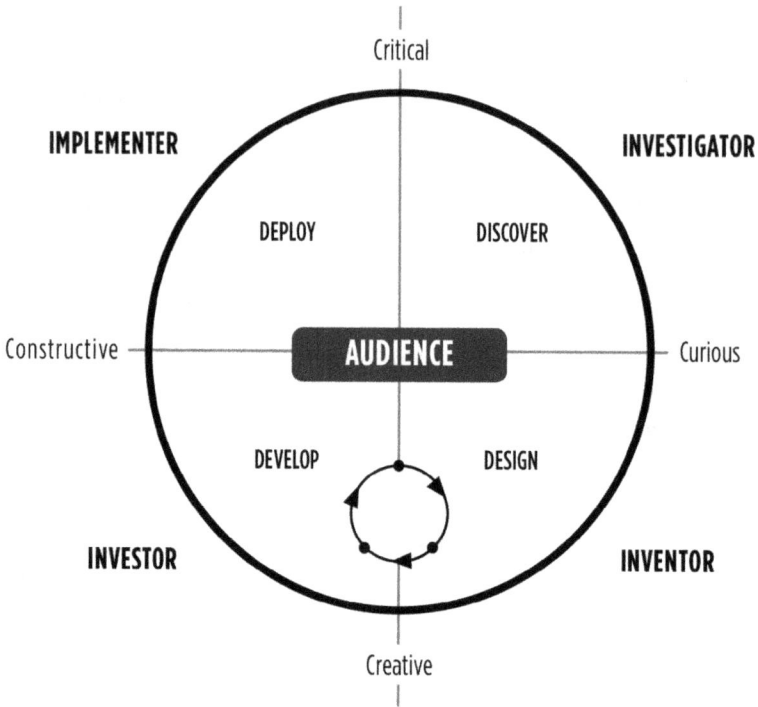

The origin of the 4D model (Discover, Define, Develop, Deliver) can be found in the content from the British Design Council, IDEO, University of Copenhagen, and others.

AUDIENCE AT THE CORE

Everything that happens in the innovation process begins with knowing your audience (or consumer or customer—the terms are interchangeable and refer to the group of people for whom you are designing innovation.) Regardless of what you call them, it's critical that you define your audience narrowly enough that its members all share a common need to be met or a problem to be solved.

For example, a summer camp director responsible for middle and high school student programs discovered that overall small group attendance is declining. If the director decided to define the audience as all middle and high school students, they are assuming that all middle and high school students share the exact same needs to be met or problems to be solved. We know that is not the case. They will need to narrow the audience to a segment within the larger whole (e.g., male high school seniors). The chance of this new, more narrow audience sharing the same need or problem increases dramatically. Honing in on profiles like these is more effective than brainstorming ideas that may meet some needs of some people while ignoring greater needs of others.

Audience plays an important role as the innovation process plays out. The time and effort you spend in each stage will be more efficient and effective when there is a clear focus on a tightly defined audience.

The First Most Important Audience

As with many organizations, your company serves numerous audiences. The more narrowly these audiences are defined into sub-audiences, the more audiences there are. Also common among many organizations, there are simply not enough people and financial resources to serve every audience with excellence simultaneously. How do you determine which audience to address first, second, third, etc.?

One approach is to list all of the audiences (there could be upwards of 20 or more, depending on the size of your organization or department) and prioritize them first by size then by significance. Size is the actual number of individuals in each group. Significance is how meaningful the audience is to your organization.

Meaningfulness may mean different things to different organizations. For one organization, it could represent how critical the audience is to its future growth. For another organization, significance could be based on the degree to which the Audience fulfills the organization's core mission and purpose. And to another, Significance may represent the impact audiences have on promoting the brand in their social circles.

To illustrate this concept, let's look at an example. A fast-food restaurant company has dozens of narrowly defined customer audiences. When it prioritizes these audiences, Soccer Moms represent an audience that is both large in population (size) and extremely important to its business in terms of sales contribution (significance). Another audience this restaurant company serves is its franchisees. One narrowly defined Franchise Audience is franchisees whose contract agreement is less than three years old. This is a highly significant audience because the future growth of the business depends on this less-tenured group of franchisees. Nonetheless, the number of these franchisees is quite small when compared to all Franchisees in the total system.

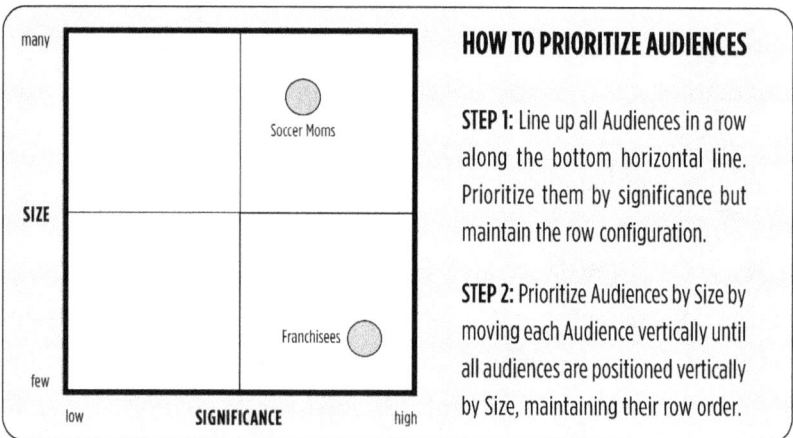

HOW TO PRIORITIZE AUDIENCES

STEP 1: Line up all Audiences in a row along the bottom horizontal line. Prioritize them by significance but maintain the row configuration.

STEP 2: Prioritize Audiences by Size by moving each Audience vertically until all audiences are positioned vertically by Size, maintaining their row order.

> **RULE:** There should be no two Audiences on the same horizontal or vertical plane. Audiences must be ranked relative to each other so that there will be Audiences positioned in all four quadrants.

After prioritizing all the audiences relative to each other, focus on those in the upper right quadrant. Select one audience from that quadrant that represents *the largest group with the highest level of significance*. That audience becomes the First Most Important Audience (fMIA). Keep in mind, this definition does not render the other audiences unimportant. To be effective, you can only focus on one audience at a time (remember, a goal of the Innovation Process is to provide clarity and focus). After you begin to take the fMIA through the Innovation Process, you can circle back to address the Second MIA (sMIA), then the third, and so on. Keep going until all the audiences in the top right quadrant have been addressed.

STAGE ONE: DISCOVER

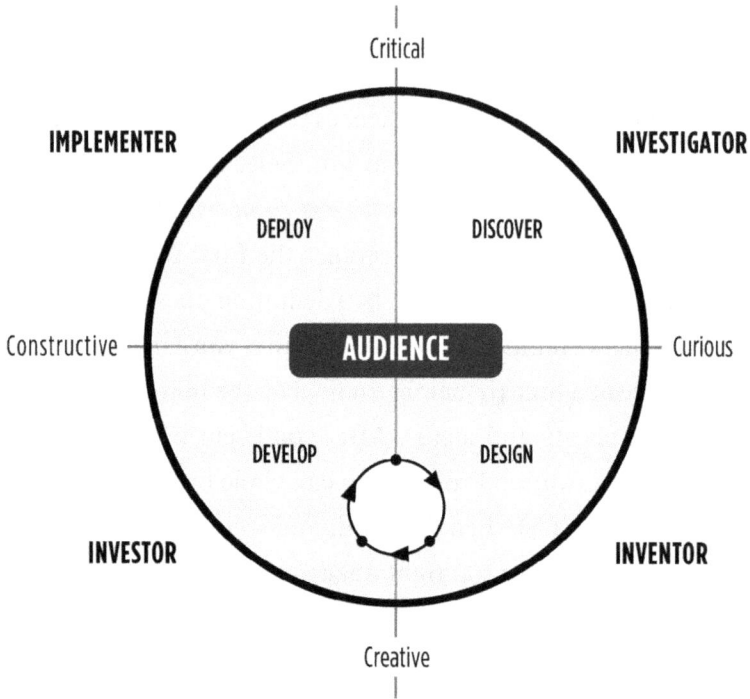

Once you have selected your fMIA, the project moves into the Discover Stage. The first task in this stage is to develop Discovery and/or Opportunity Statements. This approach is acutely audience-centric: you will determine who your fMIA is and discover the root cause of their most pressing Need, Pain, or Obstacle (NPO), and produce a Discovery Statement.

The Discovery Statement consists of four blanks. On the surface, it appears to be a simple exercise. Do not let its simplicity fool you. Each blank represents significant work. Validating the information that goes into them is critical because it sets the trajectory for everything that follows.

DISCOVERY STATEMENT

Considering [   ] (audience),

we've discovered that [   ] (needs/pain/obstacles),

which is caused by [   ] (root cause).

If solved, the benefits to the audience would be [   ].

The first blank is your fMIA. The second blank is the audience's NPO. Keep in mind that the audience will likely have more than one NPO. Discovering multiple NPOs is part of conducting productive, inquisitive conversations with the audience. How do you know which NPO to solve first? The prioritization process is like the audience prioritization exercise. This time, NPOs will be ranked first by the amount of **positive impact** solving the NPO will have on the audience, then by the amount of **effort** it will require to solve it. In prioritizing NPOs, focus on those that are in the lower right-hand quadrant because they represent the NPOs with the highest impact that require the least amount of effort. Only consider NPOs that are realistically feasible and within the team's span of control.

For example, if the Safety Team is working on improving the safety of highway construction workers and one of the NPOs from the audience of morning commuters is that there is always road construction happening on their routes, then that NPO should be removed because the Safety Team does not have control over what construction projects happen or when. The NPOs must be something you and your team have authority to actually solve.

high ┌─────────┬─────────┐   Follow **STEP 1** & **STEP 2** from pre-
     │   │   │   vious Audience exercise and
     │   │   │   apply the same Rule.
     │   │   │
EFFORT ├─────────┼─────────┤
     │   │   │
     │   │   │
     │   │   │
low └─────────┴─────────┘
       low   **IMPACT**   high

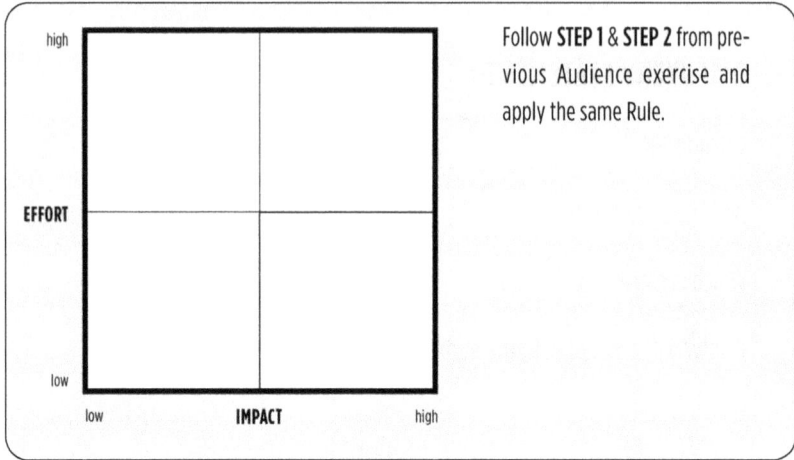

> ## *There is more to solving a problem than problem-solving.*

To be valid, this should not be what you *think* the Audience's NPO is, but rather what the Audience has *told you* their NPO is. Empathy interviews and/or empathetic observation of the audience are essential. Many organizations default to surveys because they are easier and faster. Surveys, however, do not allow for valuable probing questions such as "Tell me more about that," "Why did you take that action?" and "What are your thoughts about that?" Investing adequate time and energy into meaningful conversations with a sample of the audience will pay great dividends. The insights will be richer, and direction will be clearer.

Even if you believe you are certain you know what the NPOs are, validate your thoughts with the audience directly to confirm you are correct. If the NPO is inaccurate, then it sends the project off in the wrong direction, solving the wrong problem, and that can be both frustrating and costly.

Questions **to consider in the Discover Stage**:

➤ Are we solving the right problem?

➤ Who is it a problem for?

➤ Are we solving the root cause or a symptom?

➤ What are all the problems we could be solving and how should we prioritize the one that will have the greatest impact for the least amount of effort?

➤ How do we know?

➤ Have we attempted to solve this before?

The third blank describes the Root Cause of the NPO. Think of the NPO as an outward expression or manifestation of something deeper. If the NPO is like the symptom, the Root Cause is what must be treated to eliminate the symptom. Sometimes the audience can help surface the underlying conditions that are causing their NPO. Many times, however, the Root Cause may not be something the Audience can articulate (or is even aware of) and you may have to do more work to get to the bottom of it.

The fourth blank of the Discovery Statement deals with the value of solving this Root Cause for this audience. We call this Return On Innovation (ROI). Typically, ROI is associated with the financial return of an investment, but here we redefine the acronym to give context and measurement to the Innovation Process effort. At this point in the Innovation Process, the solution is unknown, so the investment is also unknown. It is, however, possible to describe the value of solving the Root Cause based on what the audience has told you the value of solving their NPO would be. You'll arrive at this understanding by asking audience members the question,

"If this NPO [*insert their actual need, pain, or obstacle*] was solved, what would it mean to you"?

Sometimes delivering innovation value does not begin with a problem, but an opportunity. Opportunities can be framed in much the same way as NPOs only with opportunity, we are looking more closely at the conditions surrounding what we believe could be an opportunistic idea. The Opportunity Statement helps frame opportunities in a way that paints a complete picture of the prospective condition at hand. Each blank, like those of the Discovery Statement, requires a great deal of thoughtful attention and inquiry to authenticate the condition and fully validate the cause of this condition.

The Opportunity Statement helps to add clarity and focus when exploring a new idea in much the same way as the Discovery Statement brings clarity and focus to solving a problem. Because the audience is the most important component in your Innovation Process model, their voice must be fully represented here so you have clarity about what the audience believes is the value of this opportunity.

OPPORTUNITY STATEMENT

In light of [   ] (describe the condition that exists),

we believe there is an opportunity to [   ]
(describe the opportunity that exists)

that leverages our [   ] (describe the competency, capability, or asset)

and would result in [   ] (describe the specific
value this opportunity would yield)

for [   ] . (describe the audience,
people, group, department, etc., that would benefit from the results this
opportunity, if seized, would yield)

Approach and Thinking Type

Together, these blanks take an investigative deep dive into fully
understanding all aspects of the NPO and its Root Cause. A strong
sense of curiosity is important to drive effective probing questions,
which are essential for discovering meaningful insights. Like detec-
tive work, a critical approach and analysis of new information lead
to new lines of questions. New questions lead to more questions.
Most of us are not born with the ability to ask great investigative
questions. It must be developed through training and repetition.
If you have not invested in question training, now is the time. You
would not be just investing in asking good questions, you would be
learning the art of understanding, which has a positive effect on all

your relationships. (We'll spend more time on that skill in Chapter 7—Questioning Authority.)

A critical and curious mindset is used in approaching the Discover Stage. The Thinking Type is Investigator.

The Discover Stage Process

Embarking on an innovation journey is messy and stochastic. But as the diagram below illustrates, the farther along the Discovery Stage you go, the more you learn from the questions you ask, the clearer your project goal becomes, and the sharper your focus gets. That's the goal of the innovation process—clarity and focus.

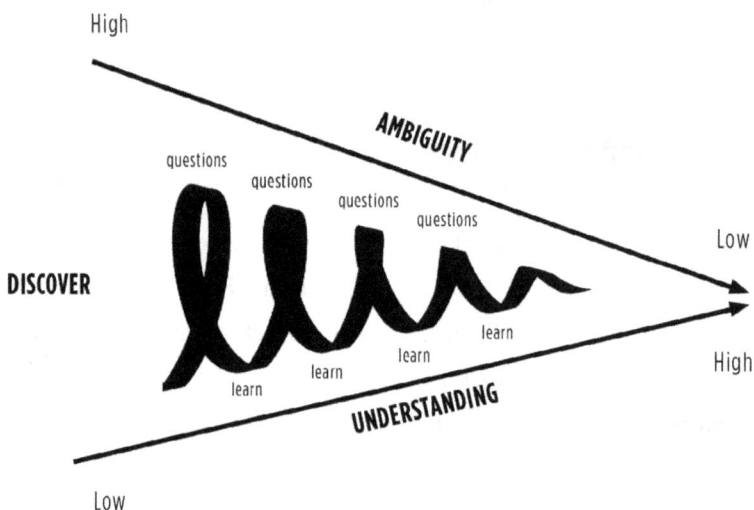

STAGE TWO: DESIGN

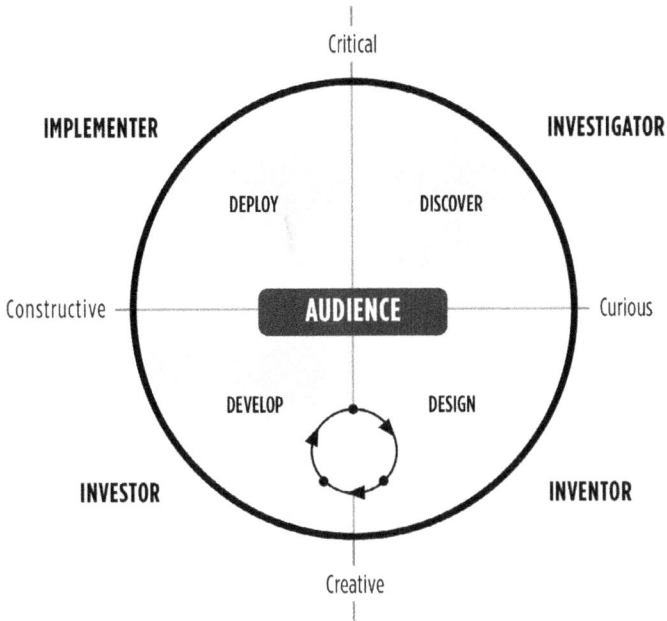

Using the Root Cause from the Discover Stage as the aiming point, you are ready to think about solutions. This stage is not a one-hour brainstorm meeting. It requires intentional planning by the leader and a commitment by the participants to be fully engaged in an event that is a departure from their everyday routine and mindset. Conditions for successful ideation sessions must meet certain criteria to create the best environment possible for the free flow of ideas. The participants must have a *focused divergence* mindset— every thought should be expressed, no matter how wild, silly, or far-fetched it may seem, while not straying from solving the Root Cause. Over the course of these one- or two-day sessions, all the ideas will be evaluated in an orderly fashion, then narrowed down to the few best possible solutions. These sessions are most productive when facilitated by an experienced ideation facilitator.

Approach and Thinking Type

It is essential that a few things are in order before you begin the design stage. First, this stage is about divergent, disconnected, unbound, wild, unrealistic ideation. A curious and creative mindset is necessary to approach this stage. Curiosity is still important but takes on a different mode of creative wonderment instead of the critical, logical, investigative line of curious questioning used in the discovery stage. What's more, the Investigator Thinking Type from the Discover Stage is not the best Thinking Type for the Design Stage. When it comes to curious creativity, the Inventor Thinking Type is the one that will contribute the most.

Planning the Ideation Session

This step begins with making sure you have **the right people** involved. Having a dominant Inventor Thinking Type does not automatically make someone great at ideation. They must be able to disconnect from the context and constraints within which they exist day-to-day to fully unleash their creative problem-solving potential. It is a good idea to include people who are Inventors but who have no skin in the game. People who have no responsibility to the audience for which you are designing will be more likely to think more creatively about solutions because their thinking is not subconsciously anchored by existing realities. An equal attendance by internal and external Inventors may give the session the best chance of yielding breakthrough ideas.

An interesting aspect of Stage Two: Design is that it brings back the Investigator and introduces the Investor Thinking Types. As mentioned above, ideas must eventually be narrowed down into only a few. Often, participants in ideation sessions feel some level of ownership of their ideas. This can emphasize biases for certain ideas based on ownership rather than the quality of the ideas themselves.

The best way to avoid this bias is to allow a non-biased idea evaluation to occur. This is a good time to bring the Investigator back into the process and ask him or her to provide feedback and thoughts. They will likely ask questions about the details related to the ideas that the Inventors have not considered. They provide a good balance to Inventors, who are all about big ideas and not so much about details. Because Investigators are all about the details, they can surface some insights that may eliminate an idea from moving forward. Also, Investors can provide an awareness of realities that must be true for an idea to realistically have a chance of launching (I'll explain that more in the next section). They are able to surface potential internal and external obstacles certain ideas will face, giving the team a more realistic perspective of an idea's feasibility. This unbiased evaluation reduces the list of potential ideas that move forward in the most effective manner possible.

The second piece that should be considered for the ideation session is to make sure it happens in **the right place**. The location and venue can make or break the ideation session because of the way our minds react to our surroundings.

Our brains have two networks: executive and default. The executive network is responsible for survival and safety. This network is "on" most of the time. It manages our daily routines and to-do lists. It is triggered by the tools we rely on, such as mobile devices, to help us accomplish our tasks every day, all day long. The default network, on the other hand, is our creative mind that produces visions and dreams of what is possible. It is associated with cognitive processes that require internally directed or self-generated thought, such as mind wandering, future thinking, perspective taking, and mental simulation. On the other hand, the executive network is engaged during cognitive tasks that require externally-directed attention, such as working memory, relational integration, response inhibition, and task-set switching. It is the part of our mind that inspires the executive mind in new ways that ultimately lead to progress.

One network is useless without the other. Unfortunately, the world in which most of us live most of the time is built and managed by the executive network. It is only when we can quiet our executive network and allow our default network to speak can we achieve our "aha" moments. This happens naturally when we sleep and dream or engage in mundane activities like taking a shower or walking in the park, which is why your setting matters so much in this process.[21]

Creating "aha" moments in an executive setting is difficult and creating an "artificial" default environment takes a significant amount of planning. If you're tasked with planning the creative session setting, start by making a list of all the characteristics of a typical, predictable meeting in as much detail as you can. You should have a list of at least 50 things. Next, consider each one by writing down its opposite. If the typical meeting uses dry erase markers and a whiteboard, for example, then use crayons and brown paper bags for your ideation session. Think "outside in." Meet at a local park, go to a nearby state park, rent an event tent in someone's backyard. Design a progressive session at different venues throughout the two days.

Finally, eliminate anything that might awaken the executive network. Tools such as smartwatches, mobile phones, laptops, legal pads, favorite pens, etc., as well as the typical everyday work attire, desks, and chairs, should be absent for your ideation session. Your goal is to give the default network space for childlike free play so it can focus on the Root Cause, unencumbered by constraints.

The third aspect that should be in place prior to your ideation session is **the facilitation** of the session itself. You should not feel obligated to lead the session. In fact, you should avoid it! There are dozens of ideation techniques that can be used. Designing an effective ideation session involves knowing which technique to employ and when. It's important that your facilitator can inspire openness and intellectual safety and gently manage participants through on-track and off-track conversations and roadblocks during these sessions. Select carefully because those are skills only experienced facilitators possess.

The facilitator will design the flow of the ideation session which could begin by having participants consider a vast assortment of ideas, reframe them, evaluate them based on predetermined design principles, then narrow them down to only a few ideas. Participants will finally refine the final ideas into workable solutions. The participants should be both exhilarated and exhausted by the end of the session. We strongly encourage you to consider employing a skilled facilitator to help ensure a successful ideation session.

The final activity of Stage Two: Design is to decide how the winning idea will be **communicated to stakeholders** who did not participate in the session. One method is to create a concept poster or one-pager that describes the idea, how it works, the problem it is designed to solve, and for whom (fMIA). This is the rough draft of the idea and the level of resolution is still low at this point, but right now, the communication does not require polish. It should be simple and detailed enough that if it were to hang in the hallway, any passerby would be able to comprehend it easily. The one-pager or concept poster is the tool you will use to communicate the idea to the audience and appropriate people within your organization during Stage Three: Develop. Many times, this tool is developed as the final activity in the ideation session and brings closure to Stage Two: Design.

Design Stage Process

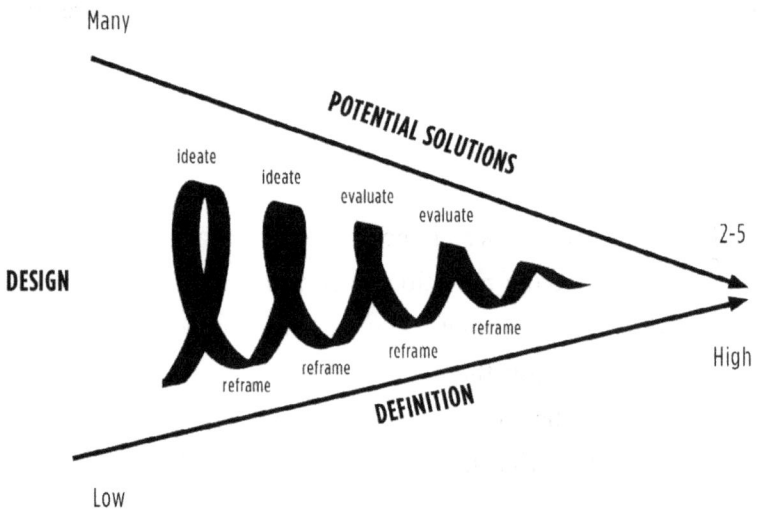

STAGE THREE: DEVELOP

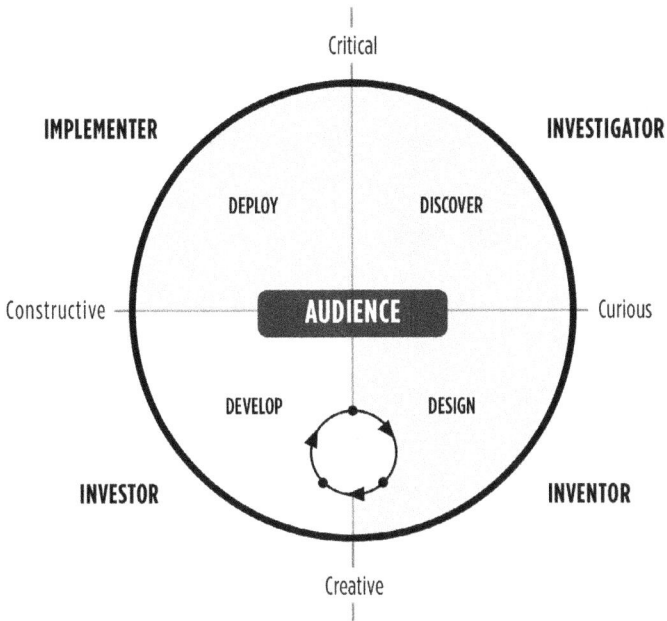

The Develop Stage is perhaps the most exciting because it is where you begin to see the idea from Stage Two: Design come to life and observe how it might solve the most important NPO for our fMIA from Stage One: Discover. Before actively developing a prototype of the idea however, you need to have completed the Prototype Readiness Checklist.

Prototype Readiness Checklist

- ☐ Receive approval from the decision-maker to proceed to Stage Three: Develop.
- ☐ Identify real-world conditions that must be true for this idea to work.
- ☐ List all assumptions about how we think the Audience will respond to this idea.
  - What will they Think?
  - How will they Feel?
  - What will they Do?
- ☐ List real-world elements that must be present for this idea to be effectively prototyped.
- ☐ Include the person or group who will be responsible for managing this idea after it launches.
- ☐ Idea aligns with the operational framework of the organization and its priorities.
- ☐ Cost is low.
- ☐ Risk is low.
- ☐ List of expected outcomes is complete.
- ☐ Consequences of unexpected outcomes are discussed in advance.
- ☐ Definition of what success looks like.

Let us look at the **Prototype Readiness Checklist** more closely and discuss the details of selected items.

Receive approval from the decision maker to proceed to Stage Three: Develop.

Defining who owns the decision for the project to move forward was discussed in Chapter Two. Here is where it comes into play. Prototyping requires resources. Someone must be in the position to make these allocation decisions and to decide whether or not to move the project forward. Responsibility for making the decision should not come as a surprise to the decision-maker. He or she should have been informed of (if not involved in) the process all along. Anticipating the required resources for prototyping is also something that should have been discussed with resource owners along the way. There should be no surprises coming out of Design and into Develop.

Identify real-world conditions that must be true for this idea to work.

If this idea were to be deployed today, certain conditions must exist for it to be successful. These conditions may or may not exist currently or, as situations within your organization change, conditions that exist now may not exist in the future. For clarity, all involved parties should be aware that for this idea to be successful, certain conditions must be true. Your job is to itemize all of these conditions. If any of them change, you have the documentation that will help either kill the idea without penalty, raise the conversation to reinstate the necessary conditions, or revisit the idea and refine it further so that a new version of it might be successful under these new conditions.

List all assumptions about how we think the Audience will respond to this idea. What will they Think? How will they Feel? What will they Do?

If you were to show the concept poster to a sample of the audience, what would they think about it? Would they recognize the NPO it is intended to solve? How do you think they would feel differently about their situation than they currently do? What actions or behavior changes would you expect from them if this idea was reality? Answering these questions will focus your work on specific assumptions and compare what you thought would happen to what actually happens when you eventually share the concept with the audience.

List real-world elements that must be present for this idea to be effectively prototyped.

Developing an idea for eventual deployment involves prototyping with a small sample of the audience. This phase entails sharing the concept poster and gathering insight that will help refine the idea. Once those refinements are made, you have the elements in place to simulate a real-life experience, but in an innovation lab setting. For example, if you are prototyping a new leadership training app, you would want to simulate how the training material would be consumed through the app. Doing so would require elements such as what the app would look like on a mobile platform and how each page would function. This simulation does not require that you create the app, only a model of how the app would work so the audience has enough of the experience to give you meaningful feedback.

Include the person or group who will be responsible for managing this idea after it deploys.

In track and field, the relay race involves four runners handing a baton to each other at specific points around the track. Of the four runners, who is the most critical? The fourth. The first runner needs to be a reliable performer and quick off the block. The second and third runners must be technically strong and able to keep the pace set by the first runner. But it is the last runner who is the most critical because they can make up time for any mistakes that may have happened along the way. The fourth position runner is the team's last chance to either maintain its lead or to gain it before the finish line is reached. Imagine if the fourth position runner had never run a relay race before, had never handled a baton, or practiced with the relay team and had no idea what was coming around the corner. A first-place finish would be almost impossible. The same is true for your project.

Your idea is the baton and the person who will be responsible for deploying and managing your new solution is the fourth position runner. To ensure a successful deployment, you need to bring this person into the process early. It is a good idea to include them from the very beginning, but it is essential to include them before prototyping starts. The person responsible for deploying the idea should have the opportunity to understand the journey the solution has been on and to buy in to it. They should have the opportunity to provide input into the prototype process and be informed and involved from this point on.

Idea aligns with the operational framework of the organization and its priorities.

The Discovery and Opportunity Statements act as guideposts in the innovation process to ensure the thinking and work stay well-aligned with the original intent and direction. Before the idea goes to prototype, you will need to ensure that it aligns with your organization's operational framework and strategic priorities. The solution will ultimately need to fit into the organizational workings of your organization.

The less disruptive the solution can be to the everyday operations the better, especially during prototyping. If the idea is strong and the problem is worth solving but the organization is not ready for it, then great care must be taken to steward the idea through the challenges of introducing it into an organization that is not expecting it. One way to manage this dance is to explain the idea only in terms of it being a prototype. Not everyone welcomes the unsettling effects that a big new idea can inflict. Talking about it as if it was a sure thing can create defensive walls that can be difficult to break through.

By conveying it as an idea that is simply being prototyped, it's less likely to be perceived as threatening. You may even say that you do not know if it is a good one, but you are exploring a new idea. Softening the edges helps prevent overreaction without cause. People are willing to hear how a "prototype" is going because the language is not threatening. Furthermore, once your idea makes it through prototyping, you will have a story to share of real impact, and that is something everyone will want to hear.

Approach and Thinking Type

Stage Three: Discover is approached best with a constructive mindset balanced by a creative attitude. The learnings that come from prototyping an idea lead to insights that improve the idea, and these learnings should be applied with the highest level of creativity. Receiving constructive feedback from your audience is like air from bellows that stoke the coals of the gold refining process—a great deal of it is required for adequate refinement.

Sometimes knowledge that comes from prototyping will send the idea back to the drawing board. On occasion, you may learn that the idea, despite numerous refinements, still misses the mark. If you do, it doesn't mean that solving the problem articulated in the Discovery Statement is no longer a worthy endeavor. What it may mean is that you need to return to the Design Stage for another round of ideation sessions.

Other times, prototyping can reveal information that you either did not have or did not consider in Stage One: Discover that calls for the prototyping to be placed on hold. When a new insight changes the direction of the project, it may be better to return to the Discover Stage where you can synthesize new data (which may lead to a new Discovery Statement), rather than continue with prototyping and attempt to force-fit the idea into a new purpose for which it was not designed.

The Investor Thinking Type is a unique blend of optimism and realism. These people will save you and your idea from fits and starts by helping you think about all the dots that need to be connected that you may not be aware of. They may come across as dream killers by introducing reasons why the idea will not succeed. Do not become defensive. This insight is absolutely critical. You cannot address or avoid roadblocks if you are not aware of them. Pull as much from your Investors as you can. Be curious and open to all the seemingly negative things they have to say. While their input can be difficult to hear, it is priceless.

Develop Stage Process

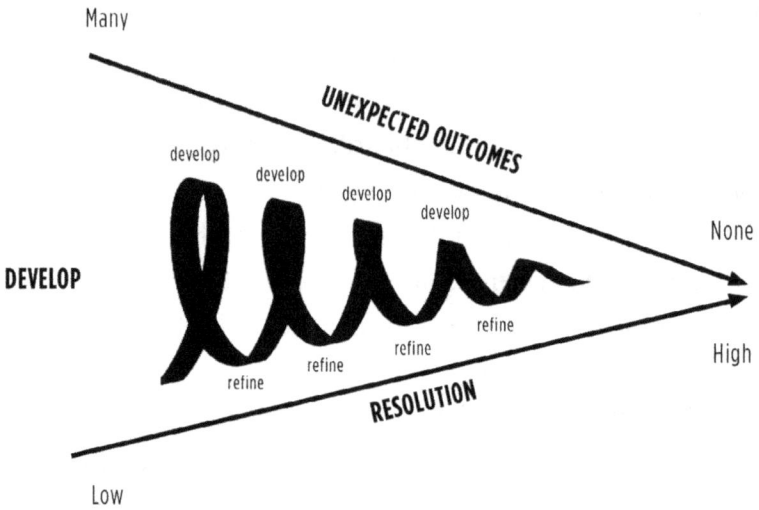

STAGE FOUR: DEPLOY

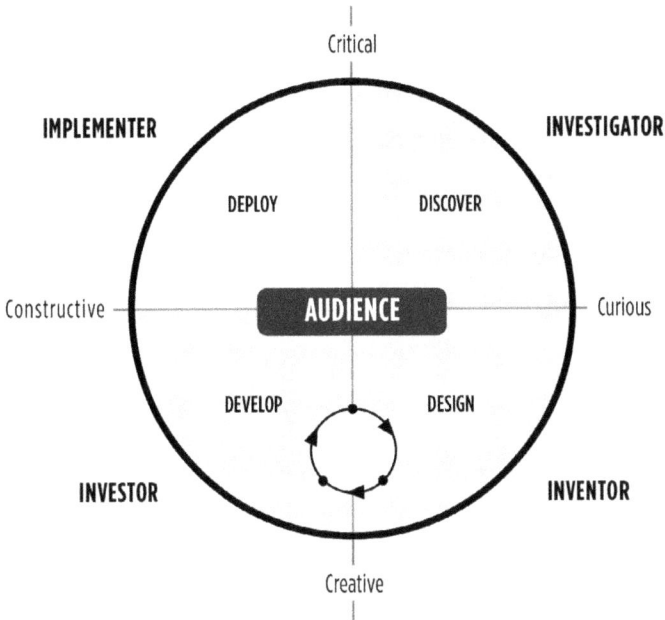

The Deploy Stage is where you begin the handoff of the idea and reach a formal end to the innovation project. Many game-changing, impactful ideas fall apart at this point. The handoff can be a long process depending on who is receiving it and the nature of the environment in which the handoff occurs. A poor handoff has immense consequences. If the person responsible for managing and maintaining the idea has been informed and involved since the Design Stage, and he or she supports the idea in its current form *and* has played a role in the progress of the idea through the Develop Stage, then the handoff should be free of significant issues. But if any of the aforementioned conditions are unmet, handing off the idea can be a long and arduous process that could compromise results. If the idea, once launched into the wild, does not deliver on the promises suggested through prototyping, it will likely be scrapped and all your time and effort will have been utterly wasted.

The most common reason for a disappointing deployment of great ideas is a simple lack of understanding. The person managing the idea must understand why:

➤ The audience is very important to the organization

➤ The NPO is very important to the audience

➤ The root cause is the reason this condition exists

➤ The solution that has been developed has been proven to solve the root cause through prototyping

When the person receiving the idea post-deployment does not understand these key aspects behind the idea, sabotage (intentional or unintentional) may occur through:

➤ Inadequate resourcing resulting in sloppy and mishandled execution

➤ Changing the idea into a more watered-down version to make it easier to manage

➤ Pushing the timeline back which can push the idea so far down the list of priorities it is forgotten and does not launch at all

Approach and Thinking Type

The mindset that should be employed at the Deploy Stage is a combination of constructive and critical. There can be many moving parts to an innovative idea and sometimes, despite your best efforts to uncover all of them in prototyping, you may discover one or two unexpected outcomes as the idea is deployed that simply could not have been simulated in the Develop Stage. Being mindful of constructive ways to make the idea better, even as it unfolds, is important. As mentioned above, the management of deploying the new innovation requires attention to detail. A critical eye for every detail involved in a rollout can help anticipate potential pitfalls such as ordering materials far enough in advance so they are available when they are needed.

The thinking type required for the Deploy Stage is the implementer. None of the other types are wired like an Implementer. This person gets things done. Period. They are keen on details, processes, flowcharts, and diagrams. They do not need much of a back story about the idea. Instead, they need to know where the goal line is and how much time is on the clock. Enthusiasm is the fuel that drives their deployment engine. You should be quite intentional to ensure your Implementer is excited about your project or they will avoid dedicating the energy it will take to deploy it well.

We've discussed how important it is for the person deploying a new idea to be supportive of it, which raises the question of whether the Implementer should be included in ideation sessions in the Design Stage. The answer is that it depends. Because Implementers are wired for action, their tendency will be to take one idea, even a partial idea, and run with it before it has had a chance to be evaluated and refined. At that point, at least mentally, they have checked out of ideating.

Participants in ideation sessions who check out can have a subtle but profound effect on the quality of the ideas. Ideation is demanding mental work and someone who is "finished" being creative sometimes carries an attitude of non-interest and disengagement, as if the work were not important. The attitude can be contagious. A facilitator worth their wages will notice this propensity and take action to correct it. This does not mean that an engaged Implementer cannot add value at the right moment in ideation. Implementers can add value when it is time to narrow the long list of ideas down to only one or two. They will know the potential challenges ideas might face when it comes time for deployment. Their distinct perspective can help inform the decision about which ideas should move forward and which should not.

In the end, whatever your process stages are called and however they are defined, everyone in your organization must **trust them**. The innovation process, derived from design thinking, has been used for centuries. It works. It always has and it always will, but only if people trust it. It is always messy at first and gray in the beginning, and there will be things that are unknown and unclear.

Just as it is with people, the process is easier to trust the more you know about it. In an innovation organization, everyone knows the innovation process. Not everyone will be experienced practitioners, but at least they are familiar with the process. For you, this means it must be taught and taught, and taught some more. New people are being hired all the time and not one of them should be onboarded without an introduction to the innovation process at your organization. This process is not just something you do—it is how you *think* about what you do. Remember, the two most important questions you can ask yourself after, "who does what?" are "am I doing the right thing?" and "am I doing things right?"

The innovation process provides answers to both. Create it, teach it, trust it!

YOUR MOVE

REFLECTION:

To what degree am I willing to commit to the innovation process we create and model the behaviors of a leader who leads with an innovation mindset by trusting it? Which thinking type is my dominant one?

REACTION:

What are the most challenging aspects of creating and implementing an innovation process in my organization? What will I do to overcome them?

ACTION:

What other innovation processes should we analyze in addition to the framework presented here as we design an innovation process that is best for us? Who should be involved internally and externally? Who owns the approval for the final innovation process design for our organization?

5

PLACE

Of all six Ps, **Place** is perhaps the most overlooked and undervalued. Your organization has a place for everything. The props from projects past are probably still stored somewhere, because that is their place. Everyone has a place to work, gather, practice, think, and so on. Place matters. Priorities that do not have a place to call their own are not priorities. Innovation is chief among all the priorities that needs its own space. Innovation as a culture and a capability may be foreign to many of your staff. They need a place to go where they can explore what innovation means and experience what it is like to do innovation and see how it works.

The practice of innovation involves communication tools such as whiteboards, easels, props for ideation, materials for prototypes, and a place to show and tell stories of innovations that have been deployed. This requires a dedicated space. It does not have to be polished and superbly finished out. In fact, it is better if it is a little raw and low-fi with a vibe that feels like something is happening there. It should not be a showcase where innovation is primarily "on display." Innovation spaces should feel like Santa's workshop, not like the hall of trophy cases in a high school auditorium. It is a maker space where energy is created and collaboration happens, where ideas are shared openly, freely, and spontaneously by everyone on staff, all within the framework of the innovation process.

Surroundings should eliminate the contextual cues of *what is* thinking and free the mind to live in the world of *what if.* Creating a vibrant innovation space does not need to cost a fortune. Design principles can be created with a simple exercise. Have someone walk around your offices and take photos of different work spaces, then post these photos and write down what you see in each photo next to it. Describe the floors, walls, ceilings (noting ceiling height), trim, lighting, colors, sources of natural light, materials such as wood, metal, etc. Next, invite others to read what has been written—without showing them the photos. Ask them to submit the emotions, feelings, and vibe that the descriptions elicit. Synthesize the descriptions of the photos and the staff's reaction to them and create themes from this information. Consider each theme individually; if there are any *what is* themes, ***do the opposite!*** For example, if one theme of your organization's interior design is "formal," a design principle for the innovation space should be "informal." The aim here is to eliminate as many *what is* questions as possible.

You may be thinking, "It would be nice to have the luxury of abundant space, but the reality is people are already having to share workstations. Where will we find space for innovation?" The question is not whether you have enough space for an innovation hub, lab, or center. The real question is, where can the feeling of innovation exist? Put on your creative problem solving hat and find a way to create a space where people can be as creative and as innovative as possible. Maybe there are design elements that can be used in a particular space when innovation work needs to happen, even something temporary that can pop up and down? Colored panels, light stands, interlocking carpet squares, mobile whiteboards, bean bags, and posters that display your organization's "stories of innovation" projects can collectively help create an innovation space where space is tight.

The point of all this effort around designing a space is to attempt to quiet the executive network in our minds and allow the default network to come alive and flourish. As you may recall from Chapter 4, Stage Two: Design, our executive network is active most of the time, especially at work! Therefore, to present our best creative problem-solving selves, we must "fool" our mind into believing that it must put the process-oriented executive network to bed and awaken the creative default network. This shift can only be accomplished by eliminating all the cues to which the executive network responds. Desks, chairs, legal pads, pens, mechanical pencils, mobile devices, laptops, wearable tech, fluorescent lighting, "work" attire, wall colors, flooring, office décor, and whatever else that may comprise what our minds interpret as work activities, to-do lists, and agendas must be removed. That should be the goal of your innovation space.

An innovation space is a required element if you hope to create a culture of innovation. One important aspect of any culture is how people relate to each other. Creating a place where staff can relate and communicate with one another and have spontaneous creative collisions with each other is essential if innovation is going to be woven into the fabric of your organization's culture.

Nothing says more about a company's commitment to be an innovation organization than the lack of an innovation space.

DESIGNING AN INNOVATION SPACE

Space can be a powerful reflection of the beliefs and practices of an innovation culture. The presence of a dedicated innovation space speaks volumes to your staff about just how important innovation is to your company. However, in the end, it also must be a space that provides a practical place to work. To create an effective, usable innovation space, consider these tips:

Flexibility and adaptability are key.

Everything should be on wheels…I mean everything! One innovation center I visited had chairs without wheels on concrete floors. Every time someone pushed his/her chair back it was like nails on a chalkboard. It was irritating and extremely disruptive. I also observed that after a team created a concept that they had mapped out on a whiteboard, they needed to share it with key stakeholders who kept very dissimilar office schedules. The challenge was, the whiteboard was attached to the wall. The team was faced with trying to preserve their work with "do not erase" signs while they tried to lure stakeholders into this off-the-beaten-path room. A whiteboard on wheels would have allowed the board to travel to a place where the stakeholders would see it no matter when they were in the office and would have freed up the wall for other teams to use.

Manage the noise.

Innovation spaces can be noisy. Help dampen sound with sonic internment materials such as carpet, theater drapes, industrial felt, acoustic tiles, etc. I was leading a Discovery workshop in an innovation lab located within a warehouse. While the teams were presenting their content, we found ourselves competing with the unusual noises coming from a nearby space. First it was animal noises, then stomping and clapping, then car noises and lots of laughing. My participants became more interested in what was going on across the warehouse than in my workshop. I was too. We decided to investigate and found that it was an improv workshop. Improv events are usually lively, and it would have been less of a distraction if the space was designed with sonic internment in mind.

Integrate unexpected details.

Unconventional lighting and sound, and unexpected visuals trip up the executive network. It does not know how to respond because these new stimuli do not fit neatly into the mind's existing constructs of interior workspaces. These signals help ignite the default network as the executive network shuts down a bit. Many organizations use colored lighting schemes, instrumental music beds in the background, and exciting unexpected visuals that depict movement and energy. Other visual cues can be large structures that are out of place. For example, Chick-fil-A's innovation center, called Hatch, includes a converted 28-foot Airstream travel trailer in its Imagine space, which is lined with dry-erase surfaces in the interior for lively conversations and ideation sessions. It also has two swings hanging from the rafters. Play is an essential component of creativity and swinging is a great way to quiet the executive network.

Dedicate quiet corners.

Create spaces where people can meet in twos and threes or work in uninterrupted solitude. While fun gathering spaces are cool and inspiring, sometimes a nice quiet spot is necessary to focus and process the outcome of a recent session or to reflect on an unfinished idea or to just plow through some heads-down work. It is a good idea to consider how both extroverts and introverts can maximize the spaces and achieve a balance between open-and-closed, large-and-small, and loud-and-quiet spaces.

Protect the innovation space.

Do not allow non-innovation meetings to happen in the innovation lab. Everyone will want to have a team or department meeting in the "cool" space. Tell them this is a making space, not a meeting space. Unless you're meeting about a specific innovation project, they will have to meet somewhere else. This lab norm should be actively protected because it tends to disappear over time. One organization constructed a fantastic innovation center. In the beginning, the innovation team was very protective of their turf and desired to preserve the "maker space" feel. Over time however, more non-innovation meetings became commonplace and eventually the innovation team sometimes found it had nowhere to meet…in its own building! Once that happens, it is difficult to change the behavior back to the way it was and reclaim the innovation space for innovation activity only.

Connect resources.

Consider having a need/want community board where people interested in contributing to other projects can collide with people who need help with their projects. There is such a community board in Harvard i-lab. Startups in the program post capabilities they need and students looking to gain experience and build their resumes by contributing their time post their skills. This method can be particularly effective in corporate environments. Many people look for opportunities to do new things beyond their day-to-day life while project teams are often under-resourced and would welcome the extra help.

Embrace the power of play.

Our minds are more free to think creatively when we are at play. It is an important component of creativity. That said, forget the ping pong table and retro video games. To introduce play into innovation spaces, many organizations install game consoles, foosball tables, pool tables, and puzzle tables. These elements quickly become furniture and fixtures, not lending any value to creativity or the innovation process. I had an opportunity to speak with the director of Starbucks Tryer Center about this topic and she confirmed that these "tools" go unused. Starbucks removed all the gaming elements and shifted to thinking about ways to introduce play throughout the entire space. Think of the space like a children's museum. Integrate fun, unexpected light and sound surprises, apparatuses people can manipulate by touch, unusual animal posters, and photos. All are examples of play that could be used to make an innovation space more engaging. It's an approach that makes more sense than compartmentalizing the idea of play and creativity to a dedicated room of its own.

Show and tell.

Create a Deploy Wall to highlight innovation projects that rolled out during the year. Celebrating deployed ideas is an important part of an innovation culture. Nothing tells the story of the value of the innovation process like showing an idea through its various stages of innovation. The more someone knows about the work it took to achieve the resulting idea, the more they can appreciate the process used (and the hard work it took) to get there. That said, exercise a bit of caution here. An expensive showroom highlighting the cool things the company has done may be a good idea, but it can be achieved inexpensively. What's important is the innovation story and celebrating the teams that made ideas come to life; not the showroom.

Leverage natural light.

The importance of natural light in creative spaces cannot be overstated. Workers in office environments with natural elements, such as greenery and sunlight, are 15 percent more creative. The same report also found that natural light is the number one desired natural element in workplace design, preferred by 44 percent of respondents.[22] The WELL Building Standard reported that, "Daylight is our most critical cue for synchronizing our body's internal clock, which can improve our mood, reduce stress, and positively impact Circadian system functioning." We are most creative when we are happy and well. Natural light contributes to our happiness and wellbeing. For more productive innovation spaces, flood them with natural light.

ADDITIONAL USES OF THE INNOVATION SPACE

A tour of the innovation space should be part of staff onboarding. It is typical for new staff to want to jump headlong into their new role, and many times the business demands it. But their work is like quicksand, and they sink deeper and deeper into their routine with each day that passes, making it more and more difficult for them to think about how they might approach their work with an innovation mindset. When onboarding new hires, include an introduction to innovation and the space where it can happen, it can be like a creative lifeline new staff can use to pull themselves out of their quicksand at any time. It also pays dual benefits—the new employee feels invited to think about his/her work more innovatively, and the company has improved its chances of sustained growth by strengthening its army of everyday innovators.

Hold staff-wide innovation immersion events in the innovation space. What better place is there to talk about innovation than in the space where it happens? Lunch & Learns, speaker series, creative thinking workshops where staff can learn more about innovation principles and how to apply them are opportunities for staff to visit the innovation space, ask questions of the innovation team, learn more about how to apply innovation to their everyday work, and hopefully leave informed and inspired.

YOUR MOVE

REFLECTION:

How can I routinely make disconnecting from my day-to-day to-do list a habit so that I can think more creatively about all kinds of things?

REACTION:

To what degree is our organization willing to carve out a space, even if it is a conference for one day a month, for innovation? How willing are we to repurpose space for innovation?

ACTION:

What are the next steps I can take to plan for a dedicated space for our staff to use for applying the innovation process to all kinds of projects and to think creatively about all kinds of things? Who can help me? How might we utilize virtual collaboration tools such as Miro and Mural when physical space is limited or in-person sessions are challenging?

6

PERMANENCE

A culture of innovation cannot be established then ignored. Like a vegetable garden, it takes a great deal of preparation. Room and space must be dedicated to it where adequate sunlight and water are easily available. The soil must be fertile and prepared to accept the seeds. Someone must be responsible for planting the seeds and caring for them as they begin to grow. Maintenance must begin at the start. Weeds will creep up and will need to be pulled. Without vigilance to prevent them, pests will feed on the plants and compromise the quality of the vegetables or eliminate them altogether. Vibrant plants will need to be pruned and their growth and expansion controlled. You have to pick vegetables at just the right time. Fertilizer needs to be added regularly to keep the soil rich. This is ongoing work!

The same is true for nurturing a culture of innovation. Do not allow your hard work of establishing a culture of innovation to be laid waste by neglect. Focused management of a thriving culture of innovation falls into three activities: Accountability, Education, and Communication.

A CULTURE OF ACCOUNTABILITY

You have probably heard that what gets measured gets managed. Innovation is no different. If the topic of innovation is out of sight, it will indeed be out of mind. Once that happens, the practice of innovation is reduced to a few people who have a natural proclivity for it but who will find it difficult to gain any ground outside of their small circle. Innovation should be a topic of regular conversation between staff and people leaders.

One of the most effective ways this occurs is to make applying innovation part of ongoing performance reviews. The annual review of innovation activities however, should not exist in a vacuum or independent of your organization's core values. When performance review topics are not grounded in the fundamental framework of an organization's purpose and core values, they can feel like bolt-on checkboxes that are not that relevant to the work. Staff need to see how innovation applies to their day-to-day work, and how their work connects to the broader mission of the organization. People leaders can then determine how well their team is leveraging innovation by describing how the use of innovation tools and innovation thinking shows up in their work.

One of the core values of Chick-fil-A is "We Pursue What's Next." This suggests that everyone within the organization can cultivate innovation right where they are. It also formally introduces the notion that it is an innovation organization and has created a culture of innovation throughout the company. It provides a foundational argument against the status quo.

CHICIK-FIL-A's CORE VALUES

We're here to serve.

Our success is predicated on the success of our Operators. As Staff, we are here to serve Operators, our customers, and to serve one another to ensure we grow our business, nurture our brand, enrich our culture, and deliver on our Purpose.

We're better together.

Our culture is built on a foundation of trust, authenticity, community, and mutual respect. Our differences strengthen us, and we know we are better together than we are alone. We are fortunate to work with extraordinary people and unite around something bigger than ourselves.

We're purpose driven.

Working at Chick-fil-A is more than just a job. Centered around a strong purpose that informs and inspires us, we are constantly seeking to have a greater impact, no matter how big or small the task.

We pursue what's next.

Relentless innovation drives our business. We look ahead to the future with courage and curiosity. We continually think beyond the present in search of new and better ways to create impact.

WE PURSUE WHAT'S NEXT: Relentless innovation drives our business. We look ahead to the future with courage and curiosity. We continually think beyond the present in search of new and better ways to create impact.

What have you observed that demonstrates forward-thinking and generating new ideas?

The company infuses innovation even more deeply into its leadership capabilities that serve as guiding principles of leadership. It calls leaders to be innovative by, "creating competitive advantages by leveraging differentiators, responding nimbly to new developments, adapting to disruptive competitors and adopting innovative ideas." Furthermore, its performance review framework includes innovation performance, helping to ensure that leaders can have meaningful discussions regarding their performance regarding innovation. It spells out what innovation behaviors look like.

PERFORMANCE DESCRIPTION
INNOVATION

Performance Descriptions

Skilled:
- Drives his/her area of the business to accelerate innovation and marketplace competitiveness
- Focuses his/her team on continuous improvement and fosters opportunities to reimagine how work is accomplished

Satisfactory:
- Leads his/her area of the business in a way that supports innovation and marketplace competitiveness
- Supports internal efforts to improve processes and prepare the business for the future

Identifying Performance

Does this individual **create competitive advantage?**

Have I seen him/her ...
- ... leverage differentiators wherever possible?
- ... demonstrate agility in the face of new developments?
- ... adapt to business disruptions?
- ... adopt innovative ideas?

Performance Descriptions

Development Needed:
- Manages his/her team with limited connection to broader efforts to innovate or enhance marketplace competitiveness
- Does not focus his/her team on innovating, inhibiting opportunities for change

Overused:
- Innovates in reaction to momentary competitive forces that are not important in the long run
- Spends too much time exploring new approaches without prioritizing current efficiency

Identifying Performance

Does this individual **drive competitive focus?**

Have I seen him/her ...
- ... incubate innovation in the team?
- ... focus the team on external developments?
- ... motivate the team to experiment with new approaches?
- ... accelerate the adoption of best practices?

The Innovator's DNA offers a more general approach to assessing how well staff are performing on innovation behaviors.

CONVERSATION FOR ASSESSING INNOVATORS POTENTIAL
Look tor Attributes and Design Experiences to Build Capabilities

INNOVATORS ATTRIBUTE

Associative Thinker	Questioning	Observing	Networking	Experimenting
Innovators discover new directions by connecting ideas across seemingly unrelated disciplines.	Innovators show a passion for challenging inquiry, often challenging the status quo.	Innovators are intense observers. Watching customers, products, technologies, and companies to gain insight.	Innovators find and test their ideas through a diverse network with widely varied specialties and perspectives .	Innovators are constantly trying new experiences and piloting new ideas. They avoid convictions and test hypotheses.

IN WHAT WAY HAVE YOU OBSERVED:

Associative Thinker	Questioning	Observing	Networking	Experimenting
• Pattern recognition across diverse topics • Ability to look across multiple technical disciplines • Intuitive and divergent • Non-linear thinking • Visionary, imaginative • Reflective	• Insatiable curiosity, digging a level deeper • Playful/humorous • Create problem statements • Voluminous question generator • Constant "If we tried this, what would happen?" • Challenges status quo • Questions provoke new insights, connections, and possibilities	• Wander, travel, and seek the movement and interaction of ideas • Open to new ideas and experiences • Not tied to a single idea or hypothesis • Opportunistic mindset that identifies gaps • Listens and probes customer	• Situationally collaborative • Collaborate with other experts depending on idea • Value others with diverging ideas and skills, and bring them to bear • Articulate in communicating ideas	• Hands-on • Focus on uncertainties to move things forward • Not afraid to kill a project (fast failures) • Open to new information—not tied to a single idea • Actively seek death blows

Jeffrey H. Dyer, Hal B. Gregersen, and Clayton M. Christensen. "The Innovator's DNA." Harvard Business Review, December 2009

EDUCATION

Ongoing Education—Knowledge Drops

Many innovation leaders create jaw-dropping PowerPoint slides about the value of the innovation process and give stunning presentations about the power of design thinking, but there are always those people within the organization who still have no clue about innovation or how to apply the process effectively. How do you maintain a culture of innovation when the reality is knowledge of innovation is a leaky bucket? You worked hard to fill those buckets initially with innovation learning and application. How do you keep them full?

> *To fight the inevitable drop in knowledge, consider knowledge drops.*

Chick-fil-A was experiencing high growth and rapid change. People were changing roles and positions on what seemed an annual basis. Maintaining innovation as a corporate capability was difficult because of the heightened sense of urgency for achieving results. Yet, teams that applied the innovation process were delivering the strongest outcomes. The key question was how to continue achieving results through applying the innovation process when many team leaders are so consumed with the demands of their current work, that they shortcut the process or ignored it altogether?

To answer this question, they began monthly **knowledge drops**. These monthly activities reinforced the principles behind the innovation process and how to apply them. The entire organization was invited. Knowledge drops included:

➤ View past TED Talks with specific topical application to the innovation process steps such as listening, designing, and prototyping, followed by a 20-minute discussion. The post video discussion was essential because it allowed attendees to apply what they had just heard. Care should be taken to ensure that the topic needs to be discussed within the context of your organization.

➤ Experience improv techniques for improving effective idea sharing. I was skeptical about the power of improv techniques at first, but after experiencing it, I am a solid convert. Do not think about improv as embarrassing fits and noises or the pressure to think on your feet in front of a crowd. Improv methods teach you how to form ideas in your head quickly and share them without your inner voice casting judgment about their quality. The techniques can also help your staff learn how to listen to the essence of an idea and then quickly add to it. It is a key skill that should not be overlooked in innovative organizations.

➤ Host Lunch & Learn speaker series with guests from inspiring innovation organizations such as Pixar, Lego, as well as community planners, artists, and non-profit executives, etc. You will be surprised who will say yes if you just ask. When you think about a speaker series, think about people outside the organization—the types of people you and your staff may not typically encounter or even agree with. Think about your key operational functions; what other teams perform a similar function but in a different industry? Hosting someone who has similar responsibilities within an outside organization for an interview can be engaging. The host can explore the innovation processes the guest uses, the challenges faced, successes, best practices, etc. within a question-and-answer setting. A discussion about the solutions the guest experimented with, and what he or she believes is coming next can unlock dynamic ideas within your staff that they may have never contemplated before.

➤ Conduct field trips or in-field studies to innovation centers of other companies to learn how they do innovation. Many companies are happy to host a tour of their innovation center followed by an informal innovation discussion. Encourage your staff to actively participate by writing down their observations during the tour so they can ask relevant questions afterward. I was hosting a tour at Hatch, Chick-fil-A's innovation center, and I noticed the group appeared to be disinterested and overtly incurious. We spent almost two hours together and no one took notes or asked interesting questions. After their visit, I had a pretty good idea of how strong their innovation culture and capabilities were.

Do not be disappointed if your events are not well attended at first. In one company, out of 2,000 employees, only an average of 40 to 60 people attend each type of knowledge drop event. Is that a success? Is it worth the effort? The answer is *yes* if the event is one of many opportunities for staff to engage in experiences that lead to greater innovation acumen. In this case, that is 40 to 60 people per month who became a stronger thread of innovation, strengthening the larger fabric of the company's innovation culture. Never stop improving and experimenting with all kinds of events. Be creative! Give yourself a three-year runway to prototype and learn. Eventually, you will find there will be regular attendees who are eager to become great innovators. Enlist them to help design and host their own events. Over time, you will be surprised how many people you have influenced. Do not give up!

> *An innovation culture needs knowledge drops because knowledge drops.*

Learning Modules—Beyond Knowledge Drops

In Chapter 3, we discussed the importance of establishing a common language. This language is established in the beginning of your organization's journey toward becoming an innovation organization. If systems are not in place to secure and preserve the language, the innovation culture you worked so hard to establish will become meaningless as its language becomes diluted and left to various individual interpretations. Ensuring that a productive innovation culture lives on requires education through learning modules.

Learning modules, like educational courses or masterclasses, are important to your education portfolio. They provide a framework for interactive training on *what* the innovation processes are at your company, *why* they are essential, and *how and when* to use them. Many companies with innovation cultures provide new employees with introductory learning modules such as "Innovation 101: the IBM way," "the Disney way," "the fill-in-the-blank-with-your-company-name way."

These modules are used during orientation to onboard new staff and reinforce that they have signed up with an innovation organization. Plan on updating learning components every two years to remain current and to present the content in ways that are relevant to your audience. (There is nothing inspiring or innovative about a learning module on innovation that looks like it was shot with a first-generation iPhone in a homogenous setting.)

Beyond an introduction to your innovation culture and capabilities, you can create brief content modules based on essential topics that staff should know if they want to be equipped to be innovators. I would recommend video formats that are no more than five minutes in length. Bite-sized content is best, especially if your audience is composed of senior leadership. Many of them, as we have learned, do not take the time to invest in their innovator-self. They do not have time for a sit-down meal—you'll want to give them a quick bite to go. Short segments are also less expensive to produce and update. If done well, these learning modules can accompany staff along their entire learning and development journey.

CREATING A COMMUNITY OF INNOVATION PRACTITIONERS (COIP)

I am assuming at this point that you have decided to create a decentralized model of innovation, where innovation is something everyone can do and is a mindset everyone should have. It follows then, that you will eventually establish a community of practitioners. In the first few years, this community may be small, and that is okay. These people are like software power users who know the technology inside and out. They have their own user groups to discuss shared learnings, shortcuts, and more, and they become known as the go-to experts for help and advice. Nurture a similar type or power user group for people who love innovation.

Innovation power users are people who desire the highest level of mastery when it comes to innovation. Why? Because they know it works. They have seen it pay dividends and they want to learn more. This group of innovation power users is your Community of Innovation Practitioners (CoIP).

Like any healthy community, members of the CoIP feel a unique sense of commonality and belonging that they cannot get anywhere else. That is what makes communities special. The more intensely focused on a subject matter the community is, the tighter the bond and the deeper the commitment of the members to preserve the health of their group. The focus on innovation can be intense because of its specialized nature. The skills members acquire over time such as facilitation of ideation sessions, performing root cause analysis, hosting improv workshops, and more are specialized. The more specialized the skills the more powerful the intellectual glue that bonds these innovators together. Their influence on your innovation culture and capability can be immense.

Someone must take responsibility for managing the CoIP. This person needs to be more passionate about creating innovat*ors* than doing innova*tion* and believe that creating effective innovators will lead to more valuable innovations.

Responsibilities of the CoIP Manager

➤ **Establish the CoIP purpose statement.** This statement is most powerful when co-created by a few innovation power users. It describes the reason why this group exists.

➤ **Articulate the benefits of being part of the CoIP and expectations of membership.** This is something that should connect well with existing organization norms, but also be unique enough to stand apart from their core work.

➤ **Map the developmental journey of members.** Purposeful personal development is the essence of why people are motivated to be members. Knowing what the developmental journey looks like provides milestones that keep members motivated and enthusiastic about the CoIP. For example, create a badge system. When they attend a training class, they get a badge. When they read a book like *Innovator's DNA* or *Questions Are The Answer*, they get a badge. When they participate in an innovation project, they get a badge. Badging should not be taken lightly. It should be a big deal that is recognized by the senior leaders. The badges should be able to be included on email signatures, pins on bags, stickers on office windows, staff profiles in the company directory, etc.

➤ **Provide badge benefits.** Rewards are motivating, and designing a reward program takes commensurate intentionality. Specific benefits should be associated with certain levels of badging. For example, after earning a certain number or certain types of badges, the member receives free membership to Innovation Leader and approval to attend their Field Studies, or a VIP pass/ticket to SXSW in Austin or the Idea Conference in Vail or visit the Disney Institute, or other innovation-related experiences.

➤ There can also be other aspects to leveling that include recognition of mastery that allows the member to do more for the CoIP. Achieving a certain level might permit the member to become an innovation trainer. Another level gives the member an opportunity to be an innovation coach—a departmental thought leader to help project teams move along the innovation process more efficiently. At yet another level, a member may become a master innovator and be given the opportunity to create next-generation content and activities for the CoIP.

➤ **Recognize CoIP members' activities and accomplishments.** What is a community without storytelling and lore? Creating a microburst experience that recognizes individuals in unique ways creates stories. Regular celebrations when someone achieves a new badge or reaches the next level up create intrinsic motivation for CoIP members. Communicating these achievements should be something as simple as a staff-wide email blast or a passing mention during a staff meeting. One company rings a huge bell that everyone on campus can hear. Another installed multicolored Wi-Fi bulbs in meeting rooms that change color when someone levels up. You could paint a prime parking spot with an innovation icon that the CoIP member can use for a week. The possibilities are endless and so are the dividends. Not only do these micro-celebrations create stories, they also create **interest**—the lifeblood of the CoIP.

COMMUNICATION STRATEGY

The adage, "out of sight, out of mind," is no truer than with the practice of innovation within an organization. Most employees within organizations do not perceive themselves to be innovative or possess the ability to think innovatively. Most are consumed with managing present challenges with a "what is" mindset. The concepts within innovation must constantly find new and interesting ways to break through the "what is" clutter and compel staff to approach their work through a "what if" way of thinking. Breaking through this clutter is no small task. It requires intentionality and creative problem solving. There are two sides to the communication coin. One side is **priority**, and the other is **publicity**.

Priority

The competition for your staff's attention can be fierce. And the larger the organization and the more complex the business model, the more difficult it is to garner staff's attention through corporate communication channels. Every department believes its message is the most urgent and most important. (Bless the person responsible for coordinating and creating internal communications. It is an incredibly difficult job. They must juggle a mountain of competing messages and map them to corporate priorities and align them with production windows that are inevitably challenged by last-minute requests.) How then, among this corporate communication procedural soup are messages of innovation supposed to break through?

The reality is, "what if" is usually on the losing side when competing with "what is" unless it has been given equal priority by the leader who decides what does and does not make it into internal staff communications. It will be imperative that this person understands you are building a culture of innovation that requires constant fueling and communication. The story of the innovation organization you are building needs to be told to the corporate communications people first. They need to support it and feel compelled to help create a culture of innovation within the corporate communications department. Prioritizing innovation stories over others will be easier to obtain when the corporate communications team believes in the value of creating an innovation organization.

Content Strategy

With the support of a senior leader and the corporate communications team in place, your role is to create great content and have it ready for publication at regular intervals. Think of it as publishing a monthly magazine about creating and sustaining an innovation organization. Last-minute ideas for articles will not cut it. Magazines require content submission sixty to ninety days in advance of the publication date. Use this as your framework and develop great content several weeks ahead of when you want it to be included in the corporate communication channels.

The best way to ensure you have a constant presence of great innovation-related content is to create a content strategy: who is your audience, what do you want them to think, feel, and do? Identify an annual theme(s), such as "leading with an innovation mindset" or "the innovation process." Identify your distribution channels and formats then consider how you might vary the channel to keep it interesting. Create a content calendar complete with rough draft and final due dates for each piece of content you prepare. Do this for the entire year so you know exactly what needs to be done by when.

Internal Publicity

The quality of the message has a great deal to do with whether the innovation story will be prioritized over other topics. Publicity "stunts" provide the corporate communications team with content that stands out from the usual single paragraph blurb. Innovation-related events like knowledge drops and "breaking news" including badge awards are good fodder for short publicity punches. These newsy maneuvers do not have to be over-the-top productions, but they do require some choreography.

Several times a year, as part of your annual communication plan, there should be content created that are standout stories presented in breakthrough ways. Producing it will require some budget for slideshows, photos, videos, animations, or other interesting presentation formats. Subject matter can range from recap videos of innovation-related events, footage of field trips, level achievement award ceremonies, and so on. The most important point here is that publicity keeps the awareness of innovation high among staff and requires an annual strategic communication plan. Preparation and planning are necessary, and resources therefore must be secured in the budgeting process.

Innovation Day

Perhaps the biggest publicity opportunity is to host an Innovation Day! This is *the* day, once a year, when everyone on staff can gather and be immersed in all things innovation at your organization. Think of it as a one-day camp for innovation. Your two main objectives for this day are to recognize current innovations in action and the people responsible for them, and to transport attendees to a different headspace through unique experiences that will spur a heightened level of curiosity about innovation and a desire to be part of it. Activities might include:

➤ Celebrate innovation projects and their teams that have launched during that year

➤ Recognize people within the CoIP who have achieved certain badges and levels

➤ Host special guest speakers

➤ Create novel attractions such as 3D sidewalk art, live mural painting, unusual music artists, unique local food or drink purveyors

➤ Arrange a keynote speech by senior leader

➤ Conduct short classes that teach innovation concepts

➤ Provide social media photo ops

➤ Construct exhibits where attendees can learn about opportunities to participate in upcoming events, badging and level, etc.

Internal publicity also includes writing key soundbite messages for key leaders to recite when they are speaking to a crowd. Make certain they are always equipped with the latest story and language to present a compelling case for innovation-related content when they are among peers. Increasing innovation awareness takes repetition. Repeated key messages from leaders reinforce the common language of the innovation culture you are working to establish. Remember, innovation is highly susceptible to being "out of sight, out of mind." Organization leaders who desire to create an innovation organization must carry the banner in many different forms continuously or a culture of innovation may never take hold.

SIGNS THAT AN INNOVATION CULTURE IS TAKING SHAPE

Innovation comes about when an employee develops, promotes, and implements new ideas which are key components of employees' innovative work behavior.

—**(IWB)** *(Janssen, 2000)*

The Innovation Report

The innovation report is the instrument that tells the comprehensive innovation story for your organization. In the beginning, the report may only be a thin booklet that highlights projects deployed in the year, the teams who did the work, and the outcome. With each year, the report should become more robust. Unless your organization has an innovation project management application, garnering information on projects requires quite a bit of digging. One way to go about it is to send a request for submissions to the head of each department and to your CoIP, who can help you gather information on projects within their respective departments. Submissions should include three to five photos of each team's work that illustrate the progress of their idea. The report can be quarterly or annually depending on the nature of your business.

Descriptions to include in the **Innovation Report** in the following format:

➤ What is the name of the project?
➤ Why is the project important? What problem does it solve?

> ➤ Who is doing the work?
> ➤ How was the innovation process applied?
> ➤ How much money has been allocated to the project?
> ➤ How much money has actually been spent?
> ➤ What was the expected outcome (value)?
> ➤ What was the actual outcome (value)?

Measuring the Value of Innovation

The most common metric for most innovation projects is its financial return, which is unfortunate. Innovations do not always initially pay off in dollars. Many times, investments in innovation provide learning that the organization can use to create value in other areas.

Take the common example of Post-it Notes. Dr. Spencer Silver, a 3M scientist, was busily researching adhesives in the laboratory. In the process, he discovered something peculiar: an adhesive that stuck lightly to surfaces but didn't bond tightly to them. He recalls, "It was part of my job as a researcher to develop new adhesives, and at that time we wanted to develop bigger, stronger, tougher adhesives. This was none of those."

What Silver discovered was something called microspheres which retain their stickiness but with a "removability characteristic," allowing attached surfaces to peel apart easily. For years, Silver struggled to find a use for his invention. But that didn't keep him from touting the merits of his creation to colleagues. He earned the nickname "Mr. Persistent" because he wouldn't give up. Meanwhile, Art Fry, another 3M scientist, was frustrated. Every Wednesday night while practicing with his church choir, he would use little scraps of paper to mark the hymns they were going to sing in the upcoming service. By Sunday, he'd find that they'd all fallen out of the hymnal. He needed a bookmark that would stick to the paper without damaging the pages. The rest is history.[23]

If the value of innovation is not always a financial return, then how should the value of innovation best be calculated? Many companies first analyze the dollars that have been invested in an innovation project. How do you know what the right amount of innovation investment should be? Answering this question causes many organizations to struggle. Should you look at marketplace data and case studies for guidance on how much your organization should be investing in innovation? Perhaps, but it should be done with a great deal of caution.

We know that Amazon outspends Wal-Mart in innovation tenfold. There have been similar comparisons in pharma, fintech, technology, and even governmental agencies. Should you use the percent of revenue these companies spend on innovation as a guide? While it is interesting, it is not very applicable because the cost of innovation in one industry may be very different from that in another. You might even know how much your competitor reportedly spends on innovation and so you invest accordingly.

The dollar amount is still not relevant because it is all about the *value* of the innovation and what that competitor is receiving from its innovation investment. If you base your organization's innovation investment on what your competitor spends, and your competitor is not reaping value from its investment because it is doing innovation poorly, then you risk overinvesting in innovation for innovation's sake and not investing to achieve your company's strategic goals.

The case for innovation should be based on value, not on dollars invested. The question executives should be asking is: **What's the**

value of innovation? Of course, the answer depends on how each innovation project defines "value." It could be anything from customer retention, employee engagement, productivity, loyalty, reducing defects, to new market penetration, or something else more exact to the organization. Identifying value measurement may be a good opportunity to ask for help in getting your innovation team a seat on the planning team. These questions are all part of overall innovation management, not a separate annual budget planning exercise.[24] An innovation scorecard should at a minimum include values for actual dollars spent, a summary of activities related to each innovation project, and the impact of each activity.

> *"When performance is measured, performance improves. When performance is measured and reported back, the rate of improvement accelerates."*
>
> −PEARSON'S LAW

Conversations

As you walk the halls of your organization, if a culture of innovation is beginning to take root, you will notice that different types of conversations are taking place in meeting rooms, offices, and hallways. The biggest difference you will hear is that more questions are being asked and fewer statements are being made. There is a tone of curiosity and less of subject matter authority. You will hopefully notice this in your own behavior and in meetings with your colleagues.

The other feature of an innovation culture you may notice is that people from different areas of the organization who typically do not cross paths are now regularly talking to one another. Networks, like the ones we have discussed in this book, have formed, and are playing a major role in creating better ideas. People in innovation cultures have conversations about work that involves a cross-functional component.

Collaboration

If you want to go fast, go alone. If you want to go far, go together.

—AFRICAN PROVERB

If there is one factor upon which all six Ps of essential innovation depend, it is surely the concept of collaboration. Recall that how strong the culture of innovation is at the sub-department level determines the degree to which a company is innovative overall. The strength of the innovation culture depends on how well teams collaborate. A sure sign that innovation is taking root is the presence of widespread collaboration.

In *Breaking Down the Barriers to Innovation—Build the Habits and Routines That Lead to Growth*, the authors found collaboration across and beyond the organization and active cross-pollinating are behaviors of the more innovative companies they studied. Through employee focus groups, the following collaboration characteristics were the responses to, "Wouldn't it be great if we…".

➤ Built cross-functional teams with expertise and viewpoints from different parts of the organization?

➤ Emphasized collective, versus individual, goals?

➤ Were transparent and frank while remaining respectful?

➤ Provided visibility and transparency on initiatives?

Imagine asking your employees, through an anonymous voting app, to score how they feel about each characteristic every time your team meets. On a 1-10 scale, where 1 is failing and 10 is excellent, how would your team score each characteristic? This survey could be a game-changing exercise. It could surface what the team believes are the barriers to collaboration. Understanding is the first step toward achieving high-performing, collaborative teams that leads to high-value innovations.[25]

Another method to assess team collaboration is a collaboration survey. Collaborative Coaching offers a free online assessment of team collaborative health.[26] It allows for real-time scoring across several dimensions. It provides a starting point for healthy team discussions. More in-depth team assessment can be discovered through tools provided by teaming experts such as The Table Group.

Remember, creating an innovation culture and capability is like creating a community garden. Everyone loves the idea and believes it will be valuable, but all too often it fails after only a few seasons. There are a number of reasons why. Even after a great start with new plant boxes, fresh soil, clean tools, and a kickoff event, people soon forget it is there. Other gardens fail because the neighbors who volunteer to participate are not instructed on how to nurture young plants, when to pick and when to prune, or how to use the tools effectively. And even others fail because only a few neighbors taste the bounty the garden produces so the garden's value goes unnoticed by most of the neighborhood. A community garden is easy to start but takes a lot of work to keep it going. The same is true for an innovation culture. The topics presented in this chapter are prescriptions for a healthy, vibrant innovation garden that will help ensure long-term success.

YOUR MOVE

REFLECTION:

To what degree am I able and willing to influence making innovation communication a priority? To what degree am I willing to devote time and energy to creating a culture of sustainable innovation?

REACTION:

What challenges will we face as an organization when it comes to giving innovation storytelling the priority that is equal to other traditional aspects of our organizational imperatives? To what degree will our Learning & Development or Training teams help with creating innovation learning modules? Who should be my partner?

ACTION:

What is the value of our innovation? When will I publish an innovation report? What roles do we need to change and/or create now within our organization to appropriately ensure innovation will be sustained and flourish long term?

SECTION TWO

SECRET ESSENTIALS

7

QUESTIONING AUTHORITY

Rather than being the smartest person in the room, be the smartest person leaving the room because of all the great questions you asked while you were in there.

"My greatest strength as a consultant is to be ignorant and ask a few questions."

—PETER DRUCKER

How important are questions? Everything that ever was, began with a question. Even the downfall of mankind in the Garden of Eden began with a question.

"Now the serpent was more crafty than any beast of the field which the Lord God had made. And he said to the woman, 'Indeed, has God said, 'You shall not eat from any tree of the garden?''"

—GENESIS 3:1

That one question planted the seeds of additional questions that followed. One led to another until the answers finally led to action, which led to God's very first question.

"Then the Lord God called to the man, and said to him, 'where are you?'"

—GENESIS 3:9

Innovations throughout history began with a question. From nautical navigation to Netflix, someone at some point asked a single question, which led to more. It is tempting to simply not ask the difficult, more provocative questions, because they are the most difficult to answer. Yet it is sometimes the most difficult questions that lead to breakthrough answers.

The consequences of unanswered questions don't compare to those that go unasked.

"Breakthroughs do not come from people who stand in the certainty of their answers, but from people who have the courage to stand in the uncertainty of their questions."

—OLIVIA FOX CABANE AND JUDAH POLLACK,
The Net and the Butterfly

According to Clayton Christensen, most business leaders view questions as "inefficient". Not surprising. Around middle school, questions began to carry negative connotations. The teacher became our most important person and knowing the answer to only his or her question became an important source of recognition and reward. We also realized that questioning the teacher about his or her questions had a negative effect, and simply answering the question became the conditioned (and safer) response. Consequently, we learned to be answer-driven and by the time we entered college, we had lost our ability to ask curious, breakthrough questions.

This conditioning of always needing to have the right answers may be good for professional advancement, but it is an innovation killer. We're experts in answers only, which makes us terrible at innovation. If we are going to be great innovators who can model the innovator's mindset and eventually create an innovation organization, we must kill the part of us that feels dutifully obligated to always have the right answers and revive that part of our minds that asks questions. We must become authorities on asking great questions—we must become **Questioning Authorities**.

> *He who thinks but does not learn is in great danger.*
>
> —CONFUCIUS

Knowers can kill innovation. Knowers are learners who stopped learning because they stopped asking questions. Knowers lead to an eventual decline in breakthrough innovations. Learners on the other hand are fueled by curiosity. Questions make learners of all of us. Learners lead innovation.

KNOWERS → Expertise → Incurious → Become poor question askers → **Breakthrough innovations decline**

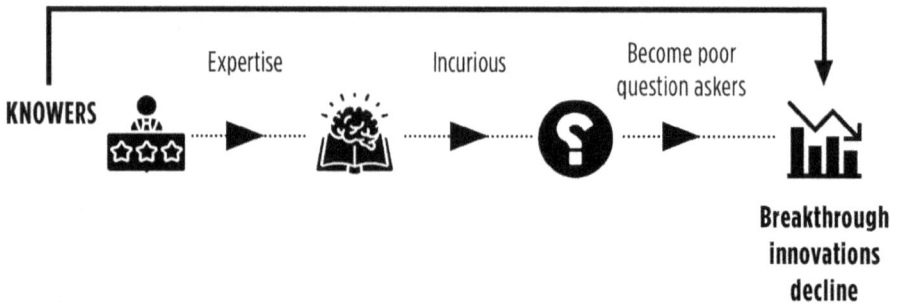

> *I believe I am only as good a leader as I am a learner, and I learn more when people trust me to be open to learning from their ideas.*

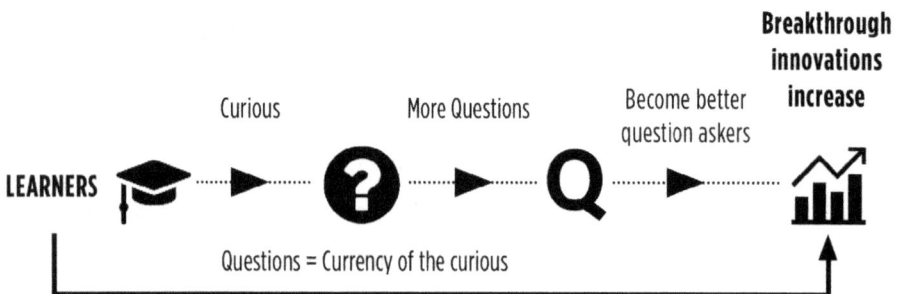

LEARNERS → Curious → More Questions → Become better question askers → **Breakthrough innovations increase**

Questions = Currency of the curious

Having the right answer is an antiquated characteristic of great leaders. In a modern world of unceasing change, there are fewer and fewer "right answers." Successful leaders of the future will be experts at asking great questions. The challenge is that great questions come from a place of naïvete, not expertise. The first question is never the best question, so ask a ton of them and eventually the best right question will be asked!

Questions lead to productive conversations. Statements, on the other hand, can lead to unproductive conversations. This can happen in one of three ways:

1. **Defend:** If the listener doesn't agree with the statement, she must defend her position

2. **Deflect:** If the statement is not aligned with the expected course of conversation, the listener may feel he must redirect it back on course

3. **Defer:** The listener postpones responding at all, thus shutting down productive dialogue

> *Questions are masters. Ideas are servants.*

EXERCISES FOR BECOMING A BETTER QUESTIONER

Gather your team for these exercises, which are designed to resolve the naïve/expert paradox. Through hands-on interactive experiences, you will learn the value of questions and understand the challenge of asking great ones. Your team will gain techniques that will help you be a better innovator, leader, and creator of a question-based culture through asking better questions.

Exercise One: Q no A

Randomly divide everyone into groups of three. For two minutes each time, a member of the small group describes a difficult challenge with a current project. The other two participants listen during those two minutes—no interruptions allowed. At the conclusion of the description, the listeners have 10 minutes to ask as many *questions* as they want (no statements allowed). The originator of the challenge remains totally silent, writing down the questions that are most striking. The roles rotate until each person in the small group has had a chance to share. (40 minutes)

Once the rotations have finished, bring everyone back to the main group and ask people to share observations, learnings, and key takeaways. (15 minutes)

This exercise demonstrates the impact questions can have on your thinking and how questions from people who are unrelated to your project can cause you to look at your project in a completely new way. It also demonstrates how to receive questions. When you receive questions without an obligation to immediately reply, it frees your mind to more thoroughly consider your answers and improve your perspective.

Exercise Two: W8

Randomly divide everyone into groups of two. The questioning partner asks the following eight questions about a project the other person is working on (it could be the same project discussed in the first exercise). If they don't have a current project to describe, the questions can relate to something the person might work on in the future, to a current process that needs to be improved, or to an obstacle they are facing. The questioning partner records the answers. Each partner has a chance to share and to record. (30 minutes)

Standard 8 Questions

1. What is the problem?
2. Who suffers most because of the problem?
3. What is the biggest pain caused by this problem?
4. Why does this problem exist?
5. Where will you find solutions?
6. Why not do something radical?
7. Who will help you?
8. When is the due date?

At the end of the 30 minutes, bring everyone back to the main group and ask people to share their observations, learnings, and key takeaways. (15 minutes)

This exercise illustrates the difference between how the free-flowing questions of the first exercise and how a more structured approach of W8 can influence your thinking in different ways.

At the conclusion of the two activities, the innovation exercise facilitator asks the large group a set of key discussion questions. There are no wrong answers to these questions. These questions are designed to ignite conversations about the role questions can play in helping your team develop their best thinking.

1. How did the first exercise differ from the second?

2. Which approach is more important? (Hint: both should be used)

3. How valuable was having someone else ask questions about your project?

4. Good questioning does not happen by itself, it takes practice. Who will be your question asking partner going forward?

> *If you don't get the question right, you won't get the answer right.*

The most enlightened people are not the ones with good answers, they are the ones with good questions.

Foster great questioning skills! Make it part of performance reviews and development discussions. Measure and track your team members' ability to ask and their inclination to do so. To become a developed innovation organization, it is essential that sub-department cultures be Q-shaped and not S-shaped. Q-shaped cultures are fueled by curiosity and are thriving question factories. On the other hand, S-shaped cultures accept traditional statement-based hierarchies as the norm. You'll make progress by employing the question-to-statement ratio and making it a routine of your conversations. As you keep asking questions and encouraging that skill in your teams, you'll become a **Questioning Authority**!

For a deep dive into asking better questions, check out *Questions Are the Answer* by Hal Gregersen, *Leading With Questions* by Michael Marquardt, and *A More Beautiful Question* by Warren Berger.

FINDING FUTURE GROWTH

How do you bridge the gap between the present day and the future? Does your organization dedicate time and attention to a method of looking into future micro and macro trends and devising appropriate plans? How much time do you or your leaders devote to future planning? Can you identify which trends really matter and which ones do not? Do you know the difference between smoke and signals? How do you know the roles you and your staff should play in future planning? This chapter discusses how to approach future planning in a way that provides practical how-to guidance.

WHY WE CAN'T GET PAST THE PRESENT

The biggest challenge in identifying future disruptions and opportunities are the necessary priorities having to do with managing the present. But our tendency to focus on the present is more than just our work being anchored to annual goals, quarterly reports, and monthly project updates.

In their book *Lead From The Future*, Mark W. Johnson and Josh Suskewicz refer to the work of psychologists and behavioral economists Daniel Kahneman and Amos Tversky, who present inherent cognitive biases that confine our thinking to the here and now and prevent us from seeing long-term opportunities and disruptions. There are more than 100 cognitive biases in the Cognitive Bias Codex.

Biases are like invisible anchors. They exist below the surface of our consciousness and prevent us from plotting new courses and exploring new horizons. Future growth depends on our ability to do future casting—to see future opportunities and steer toward them or identify future threats and avoid them. These bias anchors can keep our mindset in the still waters of the present and can fool us into believing that where we are as a company today is the best place to be in the future. That is why it is essential to be aware of these bias anchors and how each one can influence our future casting decisions. As you read the following explanation of the most common cognitive biases, think about how they might be showing up in your decision making, particularly with regard to future casting.[27]

> ➤ **Bounded Rationality** is our instinct to solve problems based solely on the information that we have immediately at hand. Future casting deals with a variety of ambiguities or "unknown knowns" and "unknown unknowns" as described by former US Secretary of Defense, Donald Rumsfeld. When we're faced with a choice of doing two projects, one of which has a set of data that helps inform our choices about the

details surrounding the project, and the other of which has very limited information, Bounded Rationality suggests we will choose the project that offers the most information.

Imagine dining at a new restaurant that has a menu with dozens of entrée choices. Subconsciously, we ignore the menu items with few or no descriptions, only attuning to those menu items that offer the most details. The future is like a menu that is devoid of description, and our tendency is to ignore it.

Another component of Bounded Rationality is the pressure we feel to make the decision quickly. The more time pressure we feel, the less likely we will fully explore all accessible information and consider every choice available.

If you have been through a quick service restaurant drive-through, you have likely experienced the time pressure component of Bounded Rationality. If there are no cars behind you in the drive-through line, you do not feel pressured to rush to an order decision. You can peruse the entire menu and consider all of your options. But if you hit the drive-through at peak rush hour, with five cars stacked up behind you, you will subconsciously feel bound to select only from the menu items with which you are most familiar.

According to Paul Boyce, time constraints constrict our ability to process and analyze a situation and come to an optimal decision. There is a natural gravitational pull from the core business that creates a sense of urgency in every decision. Future casting requires a sense of purpose, not of urgency. The urgency will increase as the future comes closer to the present over time. Until then, give future planners plenty of time and space to explore all of the variables within a variety of ecosystems in search of as much clarity as possible to make optimal decisions about future growth and profitability.

➤ *Automaticity is the ingrained habits borne of doing the same things over and over again.* A popular consumer brand had been doing the same advertising play for over a decade. I asked the long-tenured CMO what went into the decision-making process for its annual marketing plan. He responded, "When you've done it as long as I have, you just know what works."

He was subconsciously a victim of Automaticity—repeating actions that make us feel like we are making progress. Repeated actions become routines. Eventually, we repeat the routines without thinking about other possibilities. If we blind ourselves to other possibilities, then effectively forecasting future disruptions and opportunities becomes virtually impossible. Inevitably, companies operating with Automaticity bias are forced to abruptly pivot. They may face prior unseen forces that emerge and drive immediate change, or they might lose a significant opportunity. In every case, leaders are left asking, "Why didn't we see this coming?"

The mindset of future casting is rooted in exploring many possibilities (within areas of the market where the business believes it can win) to surface potential future opportunities to be seized and disruptions to overcome.

➤ *Sunk Cost Fallacy compels us to keep wasting money on losing propositions because we have spent so much on them already.* A sister concept to Automaticity, Sunk Cost Fallacy drives us to continue to do what we have always done. My Professional MBA students work for some of the most well-known, successful companies in America. When I ask them what drives decision-making in their less successful business units, many times the answer is, "We've just always done it that way."

One student I spoke with was placed in his current position for the express purpose of breaking free from the "we've always done it that way" mentality. He found it quite challenging because the company had built what it believed was equity in its ideas and did not want its investments to go to waste. The company was forfeiting growth because continuing to invest in a losing proposition was less risky than investing in an altogether new opportunity. The future *is full of new* opportunities. If we are unwilling to let go of current things to explore new opportunities, we will be trapped in the present by our own biased decisions.

> ➤ *Hyperbolic Discounting is our tendency to choose a smaller reward that we will receive sooner over a larger reward that we will receive later.*

This concept is also akin to the prior two biases. I spoke with the CFO of a company that was number one in its market, doubling the average unit sales volume of its closest competitor. The company was in high growth mode and sales trends were incredibly strong, even in the COVID-19 pandemic. Exploring future opportunities was important to the company, and even diversification through new business models was on the table. However, the CFO had to make a choice. Would the company forgo opening a new store, which would represent a sure investment with a robust payoff, or would they invest in a risky new business model opportunity, even though it could mean stronger profits long term? Which one would you choose?

The CFO decided that the company was currently making too much money from its current business model to explore other opportunities. When the company's growth curve (inevitably) flattens, will the argument against investing in new business model opportunities be that the company is not making enough money? At that point, it may be too late. Is it not more favorable to invest in opportunities, particularly risky ones, while cash flow is strong?

Hyperbolic Discounting is a powerful bias. Leaders can get to a more future forward orientation if they acknowledge the power Hyperbolic Discounting has over their decision making.

> ➤ *Normalcy Bias inclines us to overrate the likelihood of things continuing to go as they always have and to discount the possibility of them going horribly wrong.*

As the saying goes, "success breeds complacency." The longer we experience success, the more likely we believe that we will experience the same success, if not greater, in the future. Each successful year confirms our expectations of success, which is why Normalcy Bias subconsciously influences our view of the future so dramatically. If we believe that what we are doing today will be successful tomorrow, then our appetite for future exploration will not be nearly as strong as our appetite to protect what we are currently doing. This bias suffocates efforts to seek new opportunities on far-off horizons that could place the company in a position for even greater success than what it is experiencing today.

> ➤ *Confirmation Bias leads us to interpret data in a way that supports our pre-existing expectations.*

Many winning ideas have been denied the chance to become viable opportunities because the story the data was telling could not overcome the Confirmation Bias of decision makers. If leaders are not supportive of a risky business opportunity, the data surrounding a new concept must work harder to suppress their Confirmation Bias. Unfortunately, most leaders are not aware they are under the influence of this bias and are therefore unable to move past their own personal preferences and see the optimistic story the data is telling about the opportunity. Depending on how much power and influence a leader with this bias wields, this behavior can crush future casting efforts.

COGNITIVE DIVERSITY IS THE REMEDY TO COGNITIVE BIASES

In a *Harvard Business Review* article titled "Teams Solve Problems Faster When They're More Cognitively Diverse," Alison Reynolds and David Lewis define cognitive diversity as differences in perspective or information processing styles. Beyond maintaining awareness of our proclivity for these biases and of their power on us, building cognitive diversity can enhance our vision of the future and help us to progress toward future-oriented decision making.[28]

As we've already established, innovation is not only something we do, but also how we think about what we do. The same is true when considering how organizations view the future. It is not only *that* they look to the far-off future, but also *how* they think about the future that hides beyond far-off horizons.

Thinking styles play an important role in future casting. Some of us are naturally wired to seek new knowledge, generate new ideas, push boundaries, and embrace ambiguity. These are the thinking styles that make future casting more successful. Jeremy Brown and Alex Rückheim from Sense Worldwide have identified four types of people who should be part of your future casting council.

Misfits

These people contribute extreme perspectives. If you have heard someone share an idea so outlandish it made you think, "No way—that can't be done." You have probably witnessed a Misfit sharing what they believe is a completely plausible notion. Take Alan Eustice for example. By all definitions, Eustace was a geek. He was a software engineer who worked on pocket computing and computer architecture analysis tools for Digital, Compaq, and HP. He eventually joined Google, then a four-year-old startup. At Google, he worked as Senior Vice President of Engineering until he retired from that section of Google on March 27, 2015. During his career, Eustice co-authored nine publications and appeared as co-inventor in 10 patents. He showed himself to be an exemplary Misfit on October 24, 2014, when he made a freefall jump from the stratosphere, breaking Felix Baumgartner's world record. Misfits are not characterized by their profession. They are Misfits because of their extreme perspectives on what is possible. Someone who believes he can safely free-fall to Earth from the stratosphere is more likely to think expansively about the future than the sensible people around the leadership table.

Rebels

These people generate divergent perspectives. If the world says "stop," Rebels say "go." If social norms dictate certain behaviors be observed, Rebels seek their own behaviors and make society catch up to them. Martin Luther was a Rebel. Five hundred years ago, Catholics feared God and were taught that God hated mankind. The pope was believed to be the only supreme human between man and

God and only he could help humans reconcile themselves to God through offerings to the church; authority he assigned to priests as well. Luther, a priest himself, became enlightened with the realization that God did not hate mankind, but loved everyone. He pointed out discrepancies between what the Bible taught and what the church was doing. Luther taught that salvation and eternal life are not earned by good deeds but are received only as the free gift of God's grace through the believer's faith in Jesus Christ as redeemer from sin. His theology challenged the authority and office of the pope by teaching that the Bible is the only source of divinely revealed knowledge and opposed the belief that priests are meant to be mediators between God and humankind by considering all baptized Christians to be a holy priesthood. As a result of his rebellious notion, Luther became the catalyst of the 16th-century Protestant Reformation. His words and actions precipitated a movement that reformulated basic tenets of Christian belief and resulted in the division of Western Christendom between Roman Catholicism and the new Protestant traditions. Imagine someone from your own ranks presenting ideas that challenge the status quo, articulating notions that are counterintuitive to everything you were taught in school. *That* is the type of thinker who sees around corners and into the future in ways sensible people cannot.

Outliers

These are team members who have leading-edge perspectives and can clearly see innovative opportunities of the future before the rest of us. Mark Zuckerberg is an Outlier. Whether or not you like him, his business perspectives on the metaverse were leading edge in early 2020s. Building a massive communal cyberspace by linking augmented reality and virtual reality, enabling avatars to hop seamlessly from one activity to the next would a huge undertaking. It would require standardization and cooperation among tech giants who are not prone to collaborating with competitors. Zuckerberg imagined a world where the internet is something to be experienced through multidimensional and multi-sensory immersion. With a futurist perspective, he saw a world most of us cannot fathom. Beyond the capabilities of most sensible people, Outliers provide aiming points on the far-off horizon that are indicators of where the world will be taking us—an essential future casting competency.

The Crazy Ones

These are the team members who encourage disruptive perspectives to permeate their organization. They are called crazy because who in their right mind would intentionally introduce disruption into what seems to be a well-operated, successful business model? Given that your competitors are seeking to disrupt your business, you can either wait until the external disruptive pressure exceeds the force of internal resistance, or proactively rehearse possible scenarios even though it will disrupt your organization's way of operating. The Crazy Ones purposely impose disruption into parts of the business in order to protect it.

They do not see the impossibilities in their ideas. Spotify co-founder Daniel Ek is a perfect example. In an article published in *Music Business World*, Ek describes his approach, saying, "I've always done sort of impossible things. I'm naive enough to think things will always work out and I don't fully understand how hard things are." [29]

That's typical of the Crazy Ones. They thrive on presenting opposing, never-been-tried-here ideas without thinking through all the reasons why they *won't* work. Coming up with reasons an outlandish idea will not work is naturally appointed to the sensible folks around the leadership table.

You probably noticed sensible people were often mentioned as sort of a counterbalance to these other types of thinkers—almost a resisting force. While it is true that history was not made by sensible people, make no mistake, people who are practical and level-headed are essential in maintaining a strong core business. The success of any future-forward idea depends on the core business remaining strong. But gaining a new perspective that will take your organization into the future in profound ways involves connecting with Misfits, Rebels, Outliers, and Crazy Ones.[30]

A great deal of intentionality must be used as you seek the right types of thinkers with whom to engage to consider far-off opportunities. Cognitive diversity is an action that requires effort and attention. It represents the difference between being fully aware of future possibilities and mildly dismissive of what could happen someday.

If you knew what was going to be true in five years, what would you do differently this year? Would you be able to?

GETTING STARTED—GAINING EXECUTIVE SUPPORT

The most common challenge faced by future-focused innovators is the lack of executive interest. One of the most effective ways to gain leaders' support for new ideas is to meet them where they are. Often it is asking too much from executives to show them a far-off future and ask them to trust you on the journey to ambiguous destinations. The job of most executives is to ensure the results of this quarter will be better than the previous quarter. They are consumed by "today" so if you show them a bridge from "today" to "tomorrow" that begins where they are, they will feel more comfortable crossing it into the future. Use the present as a starting point.

Make the future appear to be more linked to present business objectives by connecting it to the core competencies of the business. In leaning into the things the company already does well, you help to establish common ground. From there, the discussion can lead to ways the core competencies can be leveraged and extended into potential new revenue streams. Sometimes, executives may not be aware of the core competencies of the business. This presents an opportunity for you to lead the discussion.

Discussing Your Core Competencies

The following approach can result in effective discussions around core competencies.

What are your company's strengths? If you are like most leaders, you can easily list a dozen or so. But what differentiates core competencies from strengths? That distinction is a critical point.

The Five Criteria That Define Core Competencies

1. Create value for the customer
2. Are unique or at least scarce (at a minimum in your company's industry, and better yet, in the world)
3. Are sustainable over a significant period of time
4. Are important to the company's position today
5. Can be leveraged into new products, markets, or businesses [31]

Opportunities for future growth should be explored in areas where your company can win. Core competencies help provide aiming points to such areas. As you begin to consider future growth, it is wise to strategically expand contiguously from your organization's areas of strength. If you are not accurately identifying the core competencies, it could lead to investments that are not soundly formed in areas where you can win so take care to ensure core competencies are fully vetted and analyzed. Also, core competencies can depreciate over time if not managed well or if a disruption forces your market to change and evolve in dramatically different directions. It is a good practice to routinely review your company's core competencies to understand in what ways they should be reconsidered going forward.

One way to identify core competencies is by using a radar or stargazer graph in a workshop designed to surface conversations among cross-functional leaders within the company.

Core Competency Exercise

➤ Divide cross-functional leaders into groups of five or six.

➤ Ask each person to take five minutes to write down all of the company's top strengths that he/she can think of, beginning with his/her functional area–writing one strength per sticky note.

➤ Each member then shares his/her stickies with the small group by placing stickies on a board, eliminating duplicates as each person shares.

➤ After everyone in the small group has shared, each strength is then evaluated by the five criteria discussed above. Do this by considering one strength at a time and assigning a value for each criterion based on the degree to which the strength satisfies each criterion, where 1=not at all, 2=little, 3=neutral, 4=somewhat satisfies, 5=satisfies completely.

➤ For each strength, depending on the score, the radar could look like this:

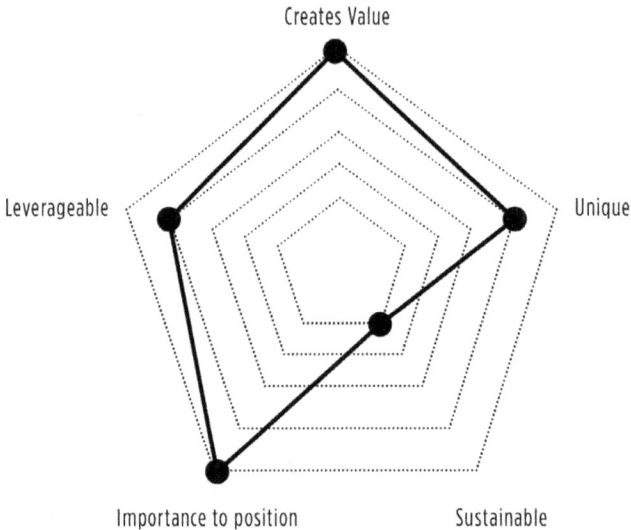

The goal for each small group is to identify which strength(s) represents the highest score for each criterion.

➤ After all small groups have completed this exercise, each group selects a spokesperson for their group who presents the group's results.

➤ After each group presents, the large group engages in a discussion about the validity and quality of the overall results. In most cases, this exercise sparks a deeper investigation into the final top strengths presented which can involve financial, competitive, consumer, market, and other analyses. These are likely more than strengths—they are core competencies. The result of such analyses is a qualified short list of no more than three core competencies. Often, companies have only one.

(See Opportunities for Growth Canvas in Appendix)

I recall one hotel chain that believed its unique guest service training model was one of its core competencies. The futurist on staff, named Jasmin, focused on trends that represented opportunities for the company to leverage this core competency in new ways. Instead of combing through mounds of broad macro trend reports, Jasmin narrowed her gaze and maximized her time by focusing on specific aiming points within the training model core competency.

Jasmin's approach led to a new business opportunity within the gig economy. She discovered that most customer complaints about their experiences with gig workers had to do with the service, not the product. Issues such as miscommunication, timing expectation, follow-through, complaint resolution, friendliness, professionalism, and working well with others represented most of the ongoing gig economy service complaints. The challenge was that companies could not provide training to gig workers directly because, under current laws, training suggested the gig worker was the employee of the company and therefore was eligible for the same benefits as full-time employees.

Jasmin believed there was an opportunity to create an online customer service training company that sold training certifications to gig workers who wished to achieve better gigs and who sought more freedom and flexibility. The model would provide subscription-based online training modules direct-to-consumer, based on existing company customer service and hospitality training content available through an e-commerce website. The platform was to be part of a third-party learning management system with which Jasmin's company already had a relationship. That bridge building opened conversations with executives who were now willing to explore what the journey across the bridge might look like.

If Jasmin would have attempted to convince executives that there is a potential opportunity on the other side of the vast canyon called the future, it is quite doubtful anyone would attempt the leap. However, starting with a current strength and describing how it can be extended across the chasm is an easier mental leap for most executives to make, and taking them across that bridge does not feel as scary.

Core competencies provide strategic aiming points from which growth might occur within areas where the company believes it has the greatest chance to succeed. They are essential as you begin to look at future opportunities. Without them, what are you scanning the horizon for exactly? There are thousands of signals out there. How do you know which ones deserve your attention? Without strategic aiming points, trends can seem too big and unwieldy. When executives cannot relate a trend or any of its signals to the decisions they need to make in the next twelve to twenty-four months, they dismiss it altogether. Remember, the way to garner support is to build a bridge from "today" to "tomorrow." It is essential to connect the core competency (today) to the relevant trend (tomorrow) that fits within the strategic aiming point.

DEFINING TREND ECOSYSTEMS

Trendspotting and future casting are often misunderstood. Many times, we focus on the hype that a trend generates through all the various media channels and overlook the numerous details that make up its ecosystem.

For example, according to PwC, there are eight technology trends shaping the world of business today, Artificial Intelligence, Augmented Reality, Blockchain, Drones, Internet of Things, Robotics, Virtual Reality, and 3D Printing. [32]

None of these trends can exist in a vacuum. Each one requires an ecosystem to support, maintain and scale it. These eight do not necessarily represent the next "wave" of innovation in and of themselves, but rather ripples that, when combined with supportive ecosystem components, might create a disruptive wave your company may have to deal with someday, or an opportunity it might seize. The rest of this chapter provides more detail around evaluating developing trend ecosystems.

THREE STEPS TO DEAL WITH TRENDS

Step One:

First, identify the various *components* of the ecosystem. This entails all of the parts that must be included in order for the trend to come to fruition. For example, in the early 1900s, when the trend of gas-powered automobiles taking over horse-drawn transportation was gaining hype there was an entire ecosystem that had to be in place before the automobile could gain marketplace momentum. Components of the automobile ecosystem included traffic laws, road signs, and signals, gasoline refining, shipping and storage, sales channels, service technician training and service locations, tools and equipment for dispensing fuel and repairing vehicles, electrical systems engineering, tire engineering and production, and more.

After all of the components have been defined, regularly analyze where each component is in its development cycle: underdeveloped, developing, or developed using a model based on the work of Rita McGrath in her book *Seeing Around Corners*:

Underdeveloped

➤ Occurring rarely, or is an expected emerging trend

➤ Infrastructure and ecosystem is unformed

➤ If the infrastructure and ecosystem begin to form, the trend could take root

Developing

➤ May be occurring now, but not widespread

➤ Infrastructure and ecosystem is in place but is newer and less structured

➤ If the infrastructure and ecosystem strengthen the trend could grow

Developed

➤ Happening now or in the near term

➤ Infrastructure and ecosystem are in place for the trend to continue growing[33]

Step Two:

Next, add each component together to determine whether the *ecosystem as a whole* is underdeveloped, developing, or developed. Simply focusing on the trend itself is too narrow of a view. For example, when Uber was gaining in popularity, focusing on the trend of crowd-sourced transportation could lead to the narrow interpretation that it could mean the end of taxis. Expanding the view to encompass the transportation ecosystem would reveal a much larger system could possibly be disrupted. We could miss the inevitable development of Uber Elevate if we only focus on taxis. Established in 2016, Uber Elevate has played an important role in laying the groundwork for the aerial ridesharing market by bringing together regulators, civic leaders, real estate developers, and technology companies around a shared vision for the future of air travel. Their software tools enabling market selection, demand simulation, and multi-modal operations are at the center of their work, and form the basis of this future-focused deal. Depending on your industry and how swiftly change is occurring, devise a rhythm of review that regularly goes through this analytical routine.[34]

Step Three:

Finally, articulate a threshold of ecosystem formation at which point you pull the trigger to create scenarios that represent possible future states and what you would do in response and/or what you would do to opportunistically pursue value. One approach would be to score components of an ecosystem across three dimensions.

Ecosystem Ranking

1. **Desirability**—To what extent do people want it enough to pay for it?

2. **Viability**—Are investors willing to invest in it?

3. **Feasibility**—Is the technology available and do policies and regulations permit it?

CHARACTERISTICS OF SIGNALS

As you consider signals of ecosystem components, ask yourself the following questions.

1. Does it provoke a different way of thinking? It is not about which tangible innovation might be successful. It is about the nature of the conversations that are influencing the necessity for a different mindset within concentrated communities of interest.

2. Conversation growth is also important. How much conversation has the topic created within the media or its original community circles? How long has that conversation been going on? How much traction does it seem to be garnering?

3. To what degree is that topic being amplified outside its original circle?

4. How many circles has it expanded to? What is the nature of those circles?

5. Most signals fail, but they fail in interesting ways. Describe its failure. What other signals in the past have failed in similar fashion and what ultimately happened to the component? Did it fade away or find a new angle of resurgence?

WHERE TO LOOK FOR SIGNALS:
INNOVATION NETWORK MAP

The mistake many organizations make regarding inventing the future is that they believe they must do it themselves through internal resources. Dr. Anna-Maria McGowan, NASA Senior Technical (ST) and Senior Executive for Complex Systems Design, reminds us, "There is no way for one company to possess the thinking and capabilities to innovate in the future."

Strategic partnerships are the key to future innovations. McGowan describes how, throughout its history, NASA has been a connector and enabler of innovators. They are not in competition with private aircraft and space organizations. They invite them to a table set with large helpings of conversation starters like, "How could the moon be a launching pad to other planets?" and then facilitate rich conversations. Your organization should do the same.[35]

By utilizing the Innovation Network Map, you can identify potential members of your network who will create rich conversations around your organization's table that could lead to new relationships and transformational innovation. Instead of hosting yet another dinner with all the predictable internal participants attending, look outside your organization and invite people who are extreme startups, opinionated enthusiasts, specialized academics, etc.

Do not forget to invite Jeremy Brown and Alex Rückheim's four types of people who should be part of your future casting council. Balance your invitation list with people who are outside of your organization but close enough to be considered "insiders."

INNOVATION NETWORK MAP

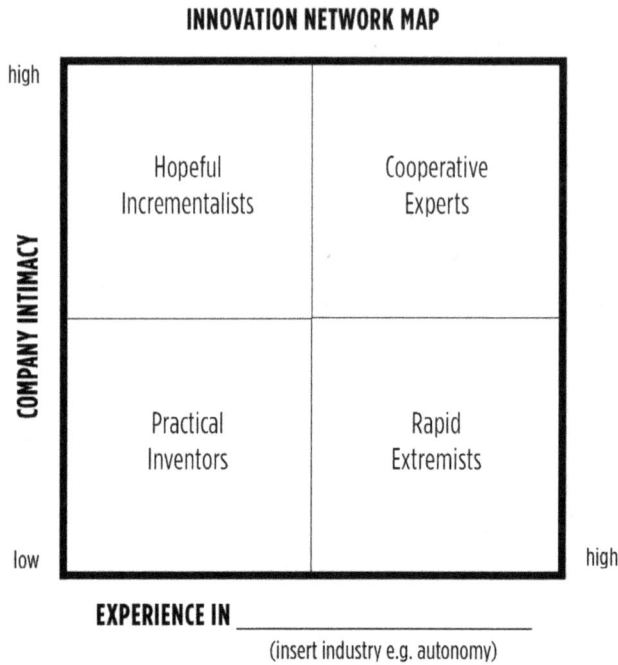

Based on NASA's model of innovation relationships

Be a connector, not a protector. Gather the right people and examine interesting topics. Allow them to interact and innovate together, and you will benefit from it. Your job is to develop and manage the process for their frequent convergence and to ensure open collaboration which could lead to a future yet unimagined.

This final chapter provided only a few approaches to analyzing and dealing with the future. How you go about searching for and identifying new opportunities or disruptions can involve any number of methods. There is no one silver bullet approach that will work for every organization. What is most important is not *how* you do it, but *that* you do it.

Every organization, for-profit, not-for-profit, and government agency needs someone on the team who can articulate a vision from a "what if" perspective and point to valuable new growth opportunities in a more far-off future. Maybe that someone is you!

APPENDIX

THE UNDERSTAND STATEMENT

PURPOSE

To provide leaders with clarity and focus.

INTRODUCTION

"A problem well stated is a problem half-solved."

Charles Kettering— Business Consultant, Inventor,
Head of Research at GM 1920-1947

REALITY

This maxim may be true regarding decision making, but its attachment to innovation is misplaced. When it comes to innovation, stating a problem well does not guarantee that the problem is thoroughly understood.

The Understand Stage of the Innovation Process is the most important stage because it sets the trajectory for the rest of the project. It also provides leaders important clarity and allows them to focus resources on work that represents the greatest impact.

FOCUS ON PRIORITIZATION

There are always more problems to solve than time and resources available to solve them. That's the purpose of the Understand Statement: **To prioritize the first most important audience and which Needs/Pains should be solved for first, second, third, and so on.**

Filling in the blanks below seems easy to do on the surface, but the work behind it is deep. Give yourself plenty of time to do this well and the chances of having to do it again will be greatly diminished. Get this part wrong and it could mean weeks or months of retooling the project because it began by solving a problem:

- that is not well understood
- with a root cause that is not a valid root cause
- that is not actually a real problem to your Audience

I. YOUR AUDIENCES

DIRECTIONS

1. List the top four Audiences that are most important to your business.

2. Define them as narrowly as possible. If the audience you have identified has different needs IN GENERAL, try to narrow the audience further until the audience represents a group of people who all share the same general needs.

3. Scoring for each audience should be done in relation to the other audiences listed. No two audiences should share the same scores for Size or the same for Significance.

4. Tiebreaker: Select the audience that represents the biggest positive impact in the business if their need was met first.

NAME	SIZE	SIGNIFICANCE	TOTAL
	1 2 3 4 5	1 2 3 4 5	
	1 2 3 4 5	1 2 3 4 5	
	1 2 3 4 5	1 2 3 4 5	
	1 2 3 4 5	1 2 3 4 5	

PRIORITY AUDIENCE *(highest total score)*

[ ]

II. THEIR BIGGEST NEED TO BE MET, PAIN TO BE SOLVED

DIRECTIONS

---

1. For the Audience identified above, list all the Needs/Pains that you have discovered through asking them directly, surveys, observation, etc.

2. Make sure these are captured from the audience, not what you THINK their Needs/Pains are.

3. MAKE IT BRIEF!

4. Scoring for each Need/Pain should be done in relation to the others listed. No two audiences should share the same scores for Deeply Felt or the same for Frequency.

5. Tiebreaker: Select the Need/Pain that, if solved, would represent the biggest positive impact in the business in the shortest amount of time.

NEED/PAIN	DEEPLY FELT	FREQUENCY	TOTAL
	1 2 3 4 5	1 2 3 4 5	
	1 2 3 4 5	1 2 3 4 5	
	1 2 3 4 5	1 2 3 4 5	
	1 2 3 4 5	1 2 3 4 5	

CAUTION

At this point, it's natural to want to think about solutions. **DON'T DO IT!**

There will be time to think about solutions in the Imagine stage. Thinking about solutions now will compromise the quality of the work you have done so far, and there's more work to be done to fully understand the Needs/Pains.

III. ROOT CAUSE OF NEED TO BE MET, PAIN TO BE SOLVED

DIRECTIONS

1. Needs/Pains are merely visible or experiential symptoms of something deeper. We're searching for that "something deeper": the **Root Cause**!

2. Ask the Audience above probing questions that begin with their highest-total scoring Need/Pain: What's causing that to happen? Keep digging until you have reached the root cause of the need/pain.

3. Make sure the Root Cause is captured from the Audience, not what you *think* the Root Cause might be.

4. There should be only one Root Cause. Keep asking "why" and other probing questions until you get there. In some rare cases, the Needs/Pains will be caused by a combination of existing conditions. Identify the one condition that, if solved for, would take care of 80 percent of the Need/Pain.

ROOT CAUSE & SCORE

How simple is this to solve this?

1 2 3 4 5

very complex   very simple

IV. THE PAY OFF: RETURN ON INNOVATION

(At least at this point)

DIRECTIONS

1. We can't provide financial projections about the return on investment (ROI) for solving the Root Cause at this point because we don't know what the solution will be. However, we can gather qualitative responses from our Audience that will assign value to this Need/Pain by a different ROI, called Return on Innovation.

2. Ask the Audience, "If this Need/Pain were solved, what would it mean to you?" We're looking for words and phrases that explain the level of meaningfulness from the Audience's perspective.

3. Unlike previous scoring, the scoring for ROI Statements can share the same score. Think of each statement along a spectrum from something that's "nice to have," to something that is "need to have." "Need to have" statements would get a 4 or 5 score.

4. Examples:

    a. Audience Response: "If this problem were solved, it would save me some time doing this task, but it's really not that big of a deal." That's a "nice to have" and would get a 1 or 2 score.

    b. Audience Response: "If this problem were solved, it would mean less stress in my life." That's big and should get a 4 or 5 score.

5. There's a chance that none of the Statements from the Audience may have a score, and that's okay. The important thing to remember is to allow the Audience to provide their statements as is, and score them as they wish. Do not try to rewrite or interpret what you think they meant. If you are unsure what they meant, ask clarifying questions.

HOW IS THIS SECTION USED?

1. It is common for a team or department to have many Understand Statements built out. The purpose of this section is to help qualify how meaningful solving this problem would be to this audience.

2. We can't solve all the Needs/Pains at the same time so we need a way to prioritize the Understand Statements. This section helps further describe how important this particular Need/Pain is to solve for our Audience, relative to all the others that also need to be solved.

RETURN ON INNOVATION STATEMENTS	MEANINGFULNESS
	1 2 3 4 5
	1 2 3 4 5
	1 2 3 4 5

V. THE COMPLETE UNDERSTAND STATEMENT

DIRECTIONS

1. Fill in the blanks using the information from Sections I, II, III & IV.

2. Add up all the scores of the previous sections to get the total score and enter it into the box below.

Considering

we've discovered

which is caused by

If solved, it would mean

TOTAL SCORE

VI. REPEAT

DIRECTIONS

1. Return to **Section II** and while still considering the same Priority Audience, go to the Need/Pain with the next highest total score and repeat **Sections III thru V** above.

2. The result will be an additional Understand Statement.

3. Continue this process until all of the Needs/Pains for this Audience have a completed Understand Statement associated with them.

4. Next, consider the next Audience with the next highest total score, and repeat the Sections II thru V: discovering Need/Pains, identifying Root Cause, and describing the Return on Innovation.

5. Repeat the process until you have prioritized all Understand Statements (the highest scoring Understand Statement is the top priority, the next highest scoring is second, and so on) for all Audiences.

UNHELPFUL BEHAVIORS OF THINKING TYPES IN DISCOVER AND DESIGN SESSIONS & HOW TO MANAGE THEM

This summary of thinking types is designed to help the facilitator understand how to manage behaviors of different thinking types in sessions or workshops so that participants are in the best mental space to add the greatest value possible.

The hypothesis is knowing one's tendency toward a dominant thinking type will make participation in collaborations more effective and lead to better outcomes. I hesitate to hard frame folks into a single thinking type because we are all able to think across all four types at any given moment. However, I would recommend you ask participants to self-select which is their dominant thinking type based on the answer to: If I had to spend all day in only one thinking type, which one would give me the most energy at the end of the day?

DISCOVER					
	Unhelpful Behavior	Outcome	Preventative Measures	Helpful Behavior	Outcome	Promotion Measures
INVESTIGATOR		The process slows down because of the Investigator's thoroughness.	Frequent verbal checkpoints where discoveries are shared and discussed.	Persistence — not being satisfied with the first, second, or even the fifth answer.	Clarity and a more thorough understanding of the root cause of the problem from the audience's point of view.	The team needs to have patience. They also need to follow the Investigator's lead and learn how they too can ask great questions driven by the answers they receive.
INVENTOR	Becomes impatient and eager to move to the Ideation stage.	Leaving the Understand stage before the root causes are clear often leads to misdirected ideation sessions and ultimately frustrating results.	Help the team by imagining new, creative questions and perhaps new ways of observing audience behaviors. Be patient. Inventors are the beneficiaries of a properly executed Understand stage.	Looks at things differently and wonders why certain things are the way they are.	Questions become more probing and observations more rich because of the different perspectives Inventors are capable of bringing to the table.	Be constantly aware of the Inventor and if they become quiet or disengaged, bring them back to the work and have them focus on the outcome that is possible.

	DISCOVER					
	Unhelpful Behavior	**Outcome**	**Preventative Measures**	**Helpful Behavior**	**Outcome**	**Promotion Measures**
INVESTOR		Leaving the Understand stage before the root causes are clear often leads to misdirected ideation sessions and ultimately frustrating results.	Frequent verbal checkpoints where discoveries are shared and discussed. Also, it might be wise to bring the Investor in at the end of the Understand stage when the insights are presented. Investors lead with questions instead of statements to give a more collaborative tone to your comments.	Having a slightly skeptical nature, the Investor could provide the extra push needed to keep digging deeper by asking "How confident are we in these answers?"	Questions become more probing and observations richer. The team feels good about the validity of its findings.	The team will need to be intentional about when to bring in the Investor during the Understand stage. Acknowledge to the team that the Investor is here to thoughtfully critique the data they are obtaining from the audience, and that this will yield the best outcome possible.
IMPLEMENTER	Similar to the Inventor, the Implementer could mentally leave the Understand stage too quickly and start planning how and when the solution, whatever it may be, will happen.	Leaving the Understand stage before the root causes are clear often leads to misdirected ideation sessions and ultimately frustrating results.	Frequent verbal checkpoints where discoveries are shared and discussed. Also, similar to the Investor, it might be wise to bring the Implementer in at the end of the Understand stage when the insights are presented.	The implementer could help ensure that work within the Understand stage is coordinated and designed to be as efficient and effective as possible.	They can help move tasks along swiftly.	If there is project management to be done, allow the Implementer to either lead it, or be a big part of it.

DESIGN						
	Unhelpful Behavior	**Outcome**	**Preventative Measures**	**Helpful Behavior**	**Outcome**	**Promotion Measures**
INVESTIGATOR	Investigators also can provide higher resolution ideas because they think through them in more detail.	Overthinking ideas can bog down the Inventor's contributions to the session.	The team (or facilitator) can give the Investigator a goal for the number of ideas they should produce, say 15 to 20. The team also brings the Investigator into the session during the narrowing down of ideas or converge section.	When engaged, the Investigator can be great at thinking in terms of "what if we did this..." and "what about this...". It leverages his/her knack for asking questions. That can be used to fuel ideation.	Raises original seeds of ideas to higher levels, making the idea better.	Use "What if..." to start thinking creatively and try to do it for as many ideas as possible.
INVENTOR	Inventors are good at ideation and sometimes it is difficult for them to shut it off once the team has selected the idea and are ready to to move on.	The team can get sidetracked by the continuation of ideating after that portion has ended.	Sometimes the best idea comes to Inventors after sharing a vast amount of other ideas. If the time for sharing new ideas is over, and you're still ideating, change your environment. If you're sitting, stand up. Try walking to a different part of the room. As you do, write your ideas down as they come to you. Eventually, the pace of thinking will slow. Review the ideas and see if there are any you feel particularly passionate about and share that one.	Generating many ideas, bringing enthusiasm to the exercise, and encouraging others to lean into ideating.	Increases the quantity of ideas for the group to consider and the space to build on them.	Prepare your mind to be "in the zone" and free from distractions. Break away from your executive neural network and allow your default network to speak freely.

DESIGN

	Unhelpful Behavior	Outcome	Preventative Measures	Helpful Behavior	Outcome	Promotion Measures
INVESTOR	Judging the feasibility of ideas in the divergent portion of the stage. This consists of both internal judgment of their own unspoken ideas, as well as the ideas of others. Also, Investors may tend to be too grounded in an approach to a particular problem and don't open up their minds to fully think in other ways.	Fewer ideas overall and even more importantly, an unsafe space to share any idea.	Write down your thoughts about your own ideas as well as the ideas of others. Be the last one to share and discern a) whether your words will be helpful to the process of creating the best solution, and b) whether your words help create safety to the open sharing of ideas.	Investors speak reality into ideas. When this is done tactfully, through process, systems and relationship related questions such as "How might this idea impact our accounting practices?" or "Will this idea compete with our drive-thru initiatives?" or "Who will be responsible for providing resources for this idea?"	Practical, critical, and valuable evaluations of ideas. This will help the team narrow down solutions to a few of the best ideas.	Questions from Investors are intended to kill ideas. Questions that are from a higher, broader, and more future-oriented perspective can bring to light some critical issues that will need to be addressed if these ideas move forward.
IMPLEMENTER	Dwells on only a few ideas because thoughts of how the idea could be launched fill the Implementer's head.	Fewer total ideas overall.	Focus on the quantity of ideas and try not to dwell on one idea for too long. Ask someone in the group to give you a subtle signal that you agree on upfront when/ if you begin to dominate the discussion.	Provides the team with helpful insights regarding potential implementation challenges as a way to narrow down ideas. Also, Implementer's knack for process can help the team get unstuck, or help them speed the conversations along in more focused, productive ways.	Provides a critical filter — considerations that will have to be addressed if a particular idea were to launch. Also, along with the Investor, the Implementer can provide a list of other parties who should be involved in order to successfully launch an idea.	Before moving to the Prototype stage, allow the Implementer time to digest the idea fully and to articulate the implications involved with its potential launch. This is a good start to developing a list of assumptions associated with a particular idea.

The four thinking types discussed in this book were inspired by the powerful Foursight Profiles work by Gerard Puccio, PhD. You can find all 15 Foursight Profiles at www.foursigh-tonline.com.

OPPORTUNITY FOR FUTURE GROWTH CANVAS

Your Name

Name the strategic opportunity:

What is the big idea we should consider?

How does this idea's value proposition work?

Circle Appropriate Number

Sales Impact (1=little, 5=significant)	1	2	3	4	5
Timeframe (1=later, 5=now)	1	2	3	4	5
Feasibility (1=low, 5=high)	1	2	3	4	5
Effort (1=high, 5=low)	1	2	3	4	5
Capability (1=all new, 5=all existing)	1	2	3	4	5

TOTAL SCORE

OPPORTUNITY FOR FUTURE GROWTH CANVAS

What are the challenges to this idea's success?

How would you rate these challenges overall: Low, Medium, High?

What are the reasons to believe this idea will work?

What micro-trend was part of your consideration? Is it Emerging, Forming, or Solidifying? *Refer to Handout*

ABOUT THE AUTHOR

Author of the 2022 book, *6Ps of Essential Innovation*, Michael McCathren is a strategic innovation expert who has spent more than 30 years leading efforts across operations, supply chain, finance, strategic planning, and marketing. At the time of this writing, he oversees Enterprise Innovation in the Innovation & New Ventures group at Chick-fil-A where he and his team are responsible for helping the organization transform its ideas into business value.

A curious, creative problem solver by nature, Michael approaches life with an innovation mindset and dedicates time to fostering that potential in others. Outside his work with Chick-fil-A, he is an adjunct professor of Innovation Management for the Terry College of Business at the University of Georgia.

Michael holds a Master of Science in Innovation from Northeastern University. He's deeply devoted to his faith and family, and enjoys seeing the world on his motorcycle or camping with his wife, Dena.

Other Titles From Ripples Media

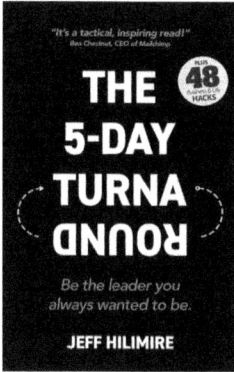

THE 5-DAY TURNAROUND

"It's a tactical, inspiring read!"
Ben Chestnut, CEO of Mailchimp

48
BUSINESS-LIFE
HACKS

Be the leader you
always wanted to be.

JEFF HILIMIRE

THE CRISIS TURNAROUND

By the Best-Selling Author of
THE 5-DAY TURNAROUND
Part of the Turnaround Leadership Series

Lead through crisis and position
your company for strength.

JEFF HILIMIRE

THE GREAT TEAM TURNAROUND

By the Best-Selling Author of
THE 5-DAY TURNAROUND & THE CRISIS TURNAROUND
Part of the Turnaround Leadership Series

How to unlock growth using PVTV™
and The Great Game of Business™

JEFF HILIMIRE

"This is the formula for how every team should run!"
—Jack Stack

Create Transformative Growth	**Lead Confidently Through Crisis**	**Putting Purpose Into Practice**
For large companies, following well-established processes is deemed necessary for securing the bottom line. But what happens when pursuing the status quo slows progress or, worse yet, creates a setback? The 5-Day Turnaround offers actionable steps for driving growth by thinking and acting like an entrepreneur, even inside mid-sized and enterprise organizations.	Most leaders plan for emergencies. But when a crisis hits, it brings unexpected challenges. In The Crisis Turnaround, Will and his team navigate disruptions to processes, projects, revenues, and teams that come as the result of an unprecedented event. The book is a case study that prepares readers to thrive in crisis and even emerge stronger.	The leadership classic The Great Game of Business (GGOB) has inspired countless organizations to operate with transparency and rigor. The first two books in the Turnaround Leadership Series introduce the Purpose, Vision, Tenets & Values (PVTV) model. In The Great Team Turnaround, these powerful concepts come together to unlock a team's unstoppable potential.

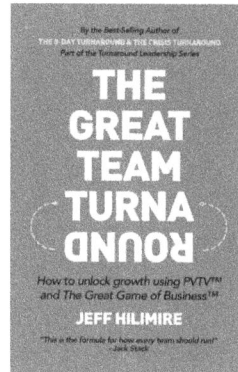

NOTES

1. Deloitte, "Building The Resilient Organization," *2021 Deloitte Global Resilience Report,* Jan. 2021: https://www2.deloitte.com/us/en/insights/topics/strategy/characteristics-resilient-organizations.html.

2. Vijay Govindarajan and Chris Trimble, *The Other Side of Innovation,* (Boston: Harvard Business Review Press, 2010).

3. Jeff Dyer, Hal Gregersen, and Clayton M. Christensen, *The Innovator's DNA* (Boston: Harvard Business Review Press, 2011).

4. Michael J. Gelb, *How to Think Like Leonardo da Vinci,* (New York: Dell, Feb. 2000).

5. Dan Pontefract, "The Foolishness Of Fail Fast, Fail Often," *Forbes,* Sep. 2018: https://www.forbes.com/sites/danpontefract/2018/09/15/the-foolishness-of-fail-fast-fail-often/?sh=68c3fa7659d9.

6. Jacob Morgan, *The Future of Work* (Wiley, 2014): https://thefutureorganization.com/books/.

7. Gary P. Pisano, "The Hard Truth About Innovative Cultures" HBR, Jan-Feb. 2019.

8. Bernadette Dillon and Juliet Bourke, "Six Signature Traits of Inclusive Leadership," (Deloitte University Press, 2016): https://www2.deloitte.com/us/en/insights/topics/talent/six-signature-traits-of-inclusive-leadership.html.

9. Basharat Javed, Sayyed Muhammad Mehdi Raza Naqvi, Abdul Karim Khan, Surendra Arjoon, and Hafiz Habib Tayyeb, "Impact of inclusive leadership on innovative work behavior: The role of psychological safety," *Journal of Management & Organization,* Cambridge University Press, Feb. 23, 2017.

10. Jim Collins, *Good to Great,* (New York: Harper Business [Harper Collins], 2001).

11. Adams Nager, David Hart, Stephen Ezell, and Robert D. Atkinson, *The Demographics of Innovation in the United States* (Information Technology & Innovation Foundation, Feb. 2016): http://www2.itif.org/2016-demographics-of-innovation.pdf.

12. Anita Williams Woolley, Christopher F. Chabris, Alex Pentland, Nada Hashmi, and Thomas W. Malone, "Evidence for a Collective Intelligence Factor in the Performance of Human Groups," *Science*, Sep. 2010: https://science.sciencemag.org/content/330/6004/686.full#aff-1.

13. Derek Thompson, "The Secret to Smart Groups: It's Women," *The Atlantic*, January 18, 2015: https://www.theatlantic.com/business/archive/2015/01/the-secret-to-smart-groups-isnt-smart-people/38462 5/.

14. Vivian Hunt, Sara Prince, Sundiatu Dixon-Fyle, and Lareina Yee, "Delivering Through Diversity" (McKinsey & Company, Jan. 2018).

15. Edgar H. Schein and Peter A. Schein, *Humble Inquiry: The Gentle Art of Asking Instead of Telling*, 2d ed. (San Francisco: Berrett-Koehler Publishers, Feb. 2021).

16. Paul J. Zak, "The Neuroscience of Trust," *Harvard Business Review,* Jan.-Feb. 2017.

17. Adapted from Clayton M. Christensen, *The Innovator's Dilemma* (Boston: Harvard Business Review Press, 2016*)*.

18. Steve Coley, "The Three Horizons of Growth," (McKinsey & Company) *McKinsey Quarterly*, Dec. 1, 2009.

19. Peter Stewart, "Teaming Anywhere: The Nine Dimensions of Successful Teaming," *Forbe*s, Mar 26, 2021.

20. Rikke Friis Dam, "5 Stages in the Design Thinking Process," *Interactive Design Foundation*, Jan. 2, 2021: https://www.interaction-design.org/literature/article/5-stages-in-the-design-thinking-process.

21. Roger E. Beaty, Mathias Benedek, Scott Barry Kaufman and Paul J. Silvia, "Default and Executive Network Coupling Supports Creative Idea Production," *Scientific Reports,* June 17, 2015.

22. Global Human Spaces Report

23. https://www.post-it.com/3M/en_US/post-it/contact-us/about-us/.

24. For more information on measuring innovation, I recommend exploring Ground Control (https://togroundcontrol.com)

25. Scott D. Anthony, Paul Cobban, Rahul Nair, Natalie Painchaud, "Breaking Down the Barriers to Innovation," *Harvard Business Review*, Nov.-Dec. 2019.

26. https://collaborative-coaching.com/team-assessment/.

27. Mark W. Johnson and Josh Suskewicz, *Lead From The Future,* (Boston: Harvard Business Review Press, 2020).

28. Alison Reynolds and David Lewis, "Teams Solve Problems Faster When They're More Cognitively Diverse," *Harvard Business Review,* March 30, 2017.

29. "The Daniel Ek Story," *Music Business Worldwide*, Feb. 21, 2021: https://www.musicbusinessworldwide.com/people/daniel-ek/?fbclid=IwAR1Qqhi6c7pTx8zSHgMD5Dq7owrjG0LZJrjKcKWGfy8LZzqtVjmIt9pCfZs.

30. Innovation Leader Master Class, "Cognitive Diversity: 5 Ways that Outliers, Misfits, Rebels, and The Crazy Ones Drive Breakthrough Innovation for Nike, PepsiCo, and SC Johnson," October, 2021.

31. Peter Skarzynski and Rowan Gibson, *Innovation to the Core*, (Boston: Harvard Business Press, 2008).

32. Find out more at www.pwc.com/us/en/tech-effect.html.

33. Rita McGrath, *Seeing Around Corners*, (Boston: Houghton Mifflin Harcourt, 2019).

34. Joby Aviation, "Joby Aviation Welcomes New $75M Investment from Uber as it Acquires Uber Elevate and Expands Partnership." Dec. 8, 2020. https://www.jobyaviation.com/news/joby-aviation-welcomes-new-75m-investment-from-uber-as-it-acquires-uber-elevate-and-expands-partnership/?uclick_id=9696ff65-2f3b-44b4-a490-cd2a3e5caad8.

35. Anna-Maria McGowan NASA Senior Technical (ST), Senior Executive for Complex Systems Design, guest speaker, Northeastern University, Summer 2021.

.

www.ingramcontent.com/pod-product-compliance
Lightning Source LLC
Chambersburg PA
CBHW071158210326
41597CB00016B/1594

* 9 7 9 8 9 8 6 0 9 5 5 1 6 *